Using Peer As
Inspire Reflection
and Learning

There is increasingly strong evidence that K-12 learners who assess each other's work and then engage in related reflections, discussions, and negotiations benefit mutually from the process. In this practical volume, Keith J. Topping provides suggestions for implementing effective peer assessment across many classroom contexts and subjects. *Using Peer Assessment to Inspire Reflection and Learning* offers pre- and in-service teachers a variety of teaching strategies to best fit their particular students and school environments along with straightforward tools to evaluate peer assessment's impact on their classrooms.

Keith J. Topping is Professor in the School of Education at the University of Dundee, UK.

Student Assessment for Educators
Edited by James H. McMillan,
Virginia Commonwealth University, USA

Using Formative Assessment to Enhance Learning, Achievement, and Academic Self-regulation
Heidi L. Andrade and Margaret Heritage

Using Students' Assessment Mistakes and Learning Deficits to Enhance Motivation and Learning
James H. McMillan

Using Feedback to Improve Learning
Maria Araceli Ruiz-Primo and Susan M. Brookhart

Using Self-Assessment to Improve Student Learning
Lois Ruth Harris and Gavin T. L. Brown

Using Peer Assessment to Inspire Reflection and Learning
Keith J. Topping

Using Formative Assessment to Support Student Learning Objectives
M. Christina Schneider and Robert L. Johnson

For more information about this series, please visit: www.routledge.com/Student-Assessment-for-Educators/book-series/SAFE

Using Peer Assessment to Inspire Reflection and Learning

Keith J. Topping

NEW YORK AND LONDON

First published 2018
by Routledge
711 Third Avenue, New York, NY 10017

and by Routledge
2 Park Square, Milton Park, Abingdon, Oxon, OX14 4RN

Routledge is an imprint of the Taylor & Francis Group, an informa business

©2019 Taylor & Francis

Library of Congress Cataloging-in-Publication Data
A catalog record for this title has been requested

ISBN: 978-0-8153-6764-2 (hbk)
ISBN: 978-0-8153-6765-9 (pbk)
ISBN: 978-1-351-25688-9 (ebk)

Typeset in Sabon
by Swales & Willis Ltd, Exeter, Devon, UK

Visit the eResource: www.routledge.com/9780815367659

Contents

1

Introduction

This chapter defines peer assessment and elaborates the characteristics of peer assessment in a typology, so you can be clear what kind of peer assessment you are talking about. Then for contrast we consider what is *not* peer assessment. The strengths and limitations of peer assessment are described. International vocabulary is discussed, leading to questions about why you should read this book and how you should read it.

What Is Peer Assessment?

Peer assessment is defined by your author as

> an arrangement for learners to consider and specify the level, value, or quality of a product or performance of other equal-status learners, then learn further by giving elaborated feedback to and discussing their appraisals with those who were assessed to achieve a negotiated agreed outcome.

Products to be assessed could include writing, oral presentations, portfolios, test performance, or other skilled behaviors.

In the olden days children might have been asked to "specify the quality" by giving a mark or grade for the assessed item. This is a kind of summative assessment, and teachers using it might be concerned about its reliability and validity. But it gives no information to the learner about how to improve. These days the second part of the definition is much more important – it is through giving *elaborated* feedback with a rationale and examples and discussing other points of view that most learning is achieved. Subsequently (and after further independent reflection), the assessee revises the work in the light of the discussion. This kind of use is clearly a type of formative assessment.

Thus, the formative view of peer assessment is emphasized here, in which students help each other identify their strengths and weaknesses, target areas for remedial action, and develop metacognitive and other personal and professional skills. Peer feedback is available in greater volume and with greater immediacy than teacher feedback. A peer assessor with less skill at assessment but more time in which to do it can produce an assessment of equal reliability and validity to that of a teacher.

You might think that elaborated peer assessment sounds rather time consuming, and initially you would be right. But during the process both assessor and assessee are presented with many intellectual challenges, set in the context of a piece of work that the assessee feels rather strongly about. As a result, both assessor and assessee have to think quite deeply, as well as negotiate a settlement, so not only are their thought processes stimulated, but their social skills as well. Consequently they *both* learn – and not just in one domain.

These practical methods are designed so all can benefit, including assessors as well as assessees, irrespective of age, ability or disability. They are: inexpensive to use, require no special materials or complex technology, are flexible and durable in a wide range of settings, and are compatible with professional instruction of almost any type.

Initially, peer feedback should highlight positive aspects of the work in question. Then it should move on to aspects that might be improved (one hesitates to say "negative"). For instance, this may involve not merely indicating the number of errors but saying exactly where they are, how they are wrong, and possibly suggesting how they might be put right. Then the pair can address features that may be errors but are open to discussion. Then the pair can discuss what aspects are missing from the product which perhaps should be there.

Peer assessment came to widespread prominence about 20 years ago, and has become extremely popular in the last ten years. You will find it in the elementary (primary) classroom and in the high (secondary) school classroom. You will also find it in the staffroom, where teachers invite peer commentary on their own efforts from other teachers. And of course you will find it among teachers in training, who solicit peer feedback on their draft assignments.

Characteristics of Peer Assessment

There are many varieties of peer assessment, and below a typology is offered that enables teachers to clearly categorize what they want to do – while reminding them of variables that they might have forgotten. It is important to be aware of what you are not doing, as well as what you are. Different kinds of peer assessment are more or less suitable for particular classroom contexts, different levels of maturity in the students, different subjects and assessed activities.

As indicated above, a key difference is whether the peer assessment is formative or summative or both. Will it serve to give students indications of how to improve their work (formative), so the final version can be better? Or will it just indicate to the students how good or bad their work was (summative), with no opportunity for improvement?

Similarly, the peer assessment can be quantitative (assigning a number with respect to a grade) or qualitative (giving rich verbal feedback on positive and negative aspects and possibilities for improvement) or both. If students are merely to give a grade, they will need considerable experience in grading before their grades can be accepted as reliable. And even if they are reliable, they do not give the assessee any clues on how to improve their work the next time. By contrast, qualitative feedback gives rich ideas on how to improve the current piece of work, let alone future pieces of work. The assessee may not agree with all of these, but some negotiation of the nature of improvement is to be expected.

Other differences between types of peer assessment are more subtle. For example, are the peer assessments on single pieces of work, or are they of several pieces of work? A piece of writing is relatively easy to assess, as it has a beginning and an end. But even here you should not assume that peer assessors are only relevant after the writing has been completed. They could, for instance, be involved as the writer tries to develop the piece of writing. Other products of work may be more complicated. For example, in peer assessment of a group presentation, should the quality of discussion prior to the presentation itself be peer assessed?

And are peer assessments on the same kind of product? The product or output assessed can vary – writing, portfolios, presentations, oral statements, and so on. Assessment of writing is very different to assessment of an oral statement, which is in turn very different to peer assessment in music or physical education. Students will need some experience of each kind of peer assessment before they have confidence that they can manage the necessary roles.

Peer assessment can operate in different curriculum areas or subjects, which may impose different demands. For example, in physical education classes, can peers be trained to investigate differences in the way the other student runs, or catches a ball, or throws a javelin, and so on? In foreign language learning, how quickly might students be able to accurately respond to the comments or questions of a peer in the foreign language?

Will peer assessment be voluntary or compulsory? Although when it is used in a class, it would be a normal expectation that all students would participate, if it is compulsory from the beginning, some students might be very resistant to participation. It might be a better idea to say that it will be voluntary at the beginning. So few students are likely to opt out that after a short while they will realize that their opposition is unusual if not a little bizarre, and agree to join in.

Will it be anonymous or not? Of course, if you have reciprocal face-to-face peer assessment in one classroom, it is impossible to make it anonymous. But if you have one class assessing the work of another class, and giving feedback in writing or over the internet, it might be much more possible. But will you actually want the feedback to be anonymous? Peer feedback from somebody you know might be more powerful than that from somebody who is anonymous.

Clarification of the assessment criteria is essential, and peers may or may not be involved in establishing these criteria. In general, peers should always be involved in the development of the assessment criteria, even if the teacher has their own ideas or there is some external assessment system that needs to be acknowledged. The fact that the peer group will eventually come up with very similar criteria to those you would have given them does not take away from the value to the peers of feeling engaged in the process. As a result, they know the criteria better from the outset.

Rubrics or structured formats for feedback may or may not be provided. Assessment rubrics almost always help the assessors and the assessees. As above, they should be developed by the peer group. But having these criteria written down will help add consistency to the peer assessment.

Training in peer assessment may be given to assessors and/or assesses to a greater or lesser extent. It is surprising how many projects in the literature appeared to give no training to the peer assessors. Some training will be needed. The only question is: how extensive will it be? It can't go on too long or the peer group will become restless to get some "real" activity. However, it should not merely involve the teacher talking. Some encounters with real life examples and some practice in actually applying peer assessment should certainly feature as part of the training.

Is any feedback provided expected to be balanced between positive and negative, or only one of these? When you are starting with peer assessment, you might be inclined to ask the peer assessors to provide only positive feedback. Then you get them used to the idea of being positive. Later, you can also ask them to give "suggestions for improvement," which, of course, are open to discussion. Once students are competent with both aspects of feedback, you can give them free rein, except that every piece of assessed work should have some positives and some negatives.

Is feedback expected to lead to opportunities to rework the product in the light of feedback, or is there no opportunity for this? When you start peer assessment, you might only have assessors giving positive feedback. Then later you can have peer assessors giving negative feedback as well. Of course, we all hope that the current version of our work is the final one, so there might be some resistance to (apparently endlessly) reconsidering (writing this book was no exception to this general rule) – although this is almost always going to result in a better piece of work. Negative feedback indicates where the work needs improving, and hopefully there will be time available to achieve this. A related question here is that of audience – why should the peer assessee try to improve the work? Who will tell the difference? Children need to see what the point is of improving the work.

Is feedback expected to include hints or suggestions for improvement? Negative feedback will be much more acceptable if it is accompanied with some suggestions for improvement, even if those suggestions are not accepted. They give the assessee something to think about, and maybe they will then come up with a completely different way of doing things.

The nature of subsequent peer assessment activity may be very precisely specified or it may be left loose and open to student creativity. Again, this may be a developmental issue, in that at the beginning, peer assessors and assessees may need a fairly strict procedure. Later, however, this may become looser, so that assessors may begin to give more feedback in their own time, as they develop a sense of responsibility towards their assessee.

Does the interaction involve guiding prompts, sentence openers, cue cards or other scaffolding devices? At the beginning of peer assessment, one, some or all of these are a good idea, as some children (especially the shy ones) will have little idea how to begin a peer assessment conversation. Giving them some questions to use if they need to get them started is an excellent idea.

The participant constellation can vary, with consequent variation in joint responsibility for the assessed product. Assessors and the assessed may be individuals, pairs or groups. Will you have one assessor and one assessee? And will their peer assessment be reciprocal? Or will you have one cooperative group assessing another cooperative group – again, reciprocal or not? Be careful in supposedly cooperative groups that all members of the group have contributed. You could invite the group to assess each of its members on the size of their contribution to the group proceedings! Then the responsibility for the finished product is not unfairly apportioned to the lazy members of the group.

Peer assessment can be one-way, reciprocal, or mutual within a group. If you have an older class assessing a younger class, directionality is likely to be one-way. If you are working with same-ability pairs in one class, directionality is likely to be reciprocal. If you are working with groups, does the group decide on a mutually agreed assessment for another group, or are the separate peer assessments of the other group to be taken into account (requiring an agreed group assessment gives the group another valuable learning experience)?

Matching of students may be deliberate and selective or it may be random or accidental. If you are new to the class it may need to be random. If you know something about the class members you can be more careful. Matching may take account only of academic factors, or also involve social differences. You may decide that you want the most able assessing the least able (not recommended). Or you may decide that you want the top half of the class assessing the bottom half of the class. Or you may decide that you want students to be matched based on having similar abilities. Or you may decide that while ability is relevant, personality and social issues are also relevant. So you may wish to avoid matching a dominant but stupid boy with a timid but clever girl, for instance.

Assessors and assessed may come from the same year of study or from different years. If you have a colleague from a class of a similar age who is also interested, you could certainly see if the two classes could be matched up for the purposes of peer assessment. If the classes are more or less of the same size, you have an ideal opportunity. But most teachers will want to experiment first within their own class.

The assessors and assessees may be of the same ability, or deliberately of different ability. If they are of the same ability, you can expect a rich dialogue between them. If they are of different ability, the flow may be more one way, with the more able child dominating the proceedings.

The amount of background experience students have in peer assessment can be very variable. Peer assessment may represent a considerable challenge to, and generate considerable resistance in, new initiates. If they have previous experience, it may have been positive, negative or both. So bear in mind the previous experience that these students might have had in previous classes. You might want to ask them about that right at the beginning.

Students from different cultural backgrounds may be very different in acceptance of peer assessment. In particular, students from a Middle Eastern or Asian background may have great difficulty accepting peer assessment. In the case of Middle Eastern students, resistance has a lot to do with gender, as boys might be very reluctant to accept advice from a girl. In the case of Asian students, the idea that there is not one right answer can be rather startling, and also lead to resistances.

Gender may thus make a difference, and thought should be given to the implications of same-sex or cross-sex matching. With Middle Eastern students, same-sex matching might be easier to start with. We have some evidence from peer tutoring that same-sex matching is generally more effective for boys, but of course that leaves you with the question of what to do with the girls. So there is no easy answer here. Of course, if there is no face-to-face contact (as in an online environment or perhaps where you have peer assessment between classes of different ages), gender may not be apparent, but this raises yet another source of variation.

Place can vary: most peer assessment is structured and occurs in class, but it can also be informal and occur outside of class. Once students become really involved in it, you may find they are having peer assessment conversations in break time. And indeed in some cases, taking peer assessment into their homes and using it with older and younger siblings.

Similar variation occurs with respect to the time when the peer assessment takes place: How long are the sessions, how many sessions? Generally the morning is best for thinking activities, but maybe peer assessment could also fit into the afternoon when the timetable perhaps feels a little looser. If a big and complicated piece of work is being peer assessed, a good deal of time might be needed, but this should be broken into smaller sections of no longer than one period, and some structure provided so that students do not go off track. Make sure you give enough time so that the peer assessment is actually finished in the time specified.

The objectives for the exercise may vary – the teacher may target cognitive and/or metacognitive gains, or teacher time saving, or other goals. We hope that the teacher will mainly target cognitive and/or metacognitive gains, but there may be other gains, such as social gains or attitudinal gains. Do you see peer assessors and assessees talking more in the playground? Do you feel that some students are more engaged in what they are doing as a result of peer assessment?

What degree of justification for opinions is expected of the assessor? In the beginning it will be hard enough to get peer assessors to give suggestions for improvement, without expecting them to say why they think what they think. But with experience, peer assessors may become more adept at this – and also be more careful about not giving an opinion until they are sure they can justify it.

Will all peer assessments be confidential to the assessing pair and the teacher, or will they be made publicly available? At the start you will want to keep the peer assessments confidential to each assessing group and yourself. Once you have checked some of them for reliability, and you are satisfied about reliability, you may wish to operate a more open system. This could of course become competitive, and you would not wish what you had hoped would be a positive social experience degenerate into a competition, but then that is up to you . . .

Another issue is the extent to which the process of peer assessment is monitored by supervisory staff. With peer assessment in one class, it is relatively easy for the teacher to keep an eye on the situation. But peer assessment between classes can become tricky in terms of keeping an eye on the situation. Obviously, you will want to be alert to any problems and able to nip them in the bud.

The extent to which the reliability and validity of the peer assessment is moderated by supervising teachers is also an issue.

While this generally comes up mainly with summative quantitative peer assessment, it can also be relevant where students are giving elaborated verbal feedback. Sometimes this may seem so off the wall that you are tempted to intervene – but remember, it is for the assessee to comment first, so give them the chance to say that the peer assessment is nonsense.

Inspecting a sample of the assessments is particularly important where the assessment is summative. Is the task a simple surface task requiring limited cognitive engagement, or a highly complex task requiring considerable inference of the part of assesses, or does a simple initial task develop into increasingly complex tasks? If it is complex you might be particularly inclined to pay some attention to the process.

In relation to this, what quantity and quality of feedback is expected, and is this elaborated and specific, or more concise and general? Time will be a major factor here. Initially you might want to ask your assessors to give two positive points of feedback and two negative points. Do you want to also ask for two suggestions for improvement? Should this be about a minute point (such as a spelling) or much broader (such as the structure of a piece of writing), or do you want to say that one should be broad but the other can be small?

To what extent is the feedback tending toward the objective and definitive, as it might be in response to a simple task, or to what extent more subjective, as it might be with a more complex task? What effect might this have on the amount of disputation that ensues? Is there time for the assessees to actually make all the suggested improvements?

How are assessees expected to respond to feedback; are their revisions to be none, few or many, simple or complex? Again, given the time constraints, you may wish to put some sort of quota on this – perhaps a maximum of three revisions to be done in 20 minutes, or some such.

What extrinsic or intrinsic rewards are made available for participants? The US has been much criticized for its use of extrinsic rewards, to the point that American students seem incapable of doing anything without getting a pizza in return. Of course, this is an exaggeration, but this is an issue the teacher must address. It is worth thinking about what the students might get out of peer assessment in intrinsic terms. Once over their first shock, do the assessors get more pride in what they are doing, more involvement as they engage their assessee(s) in conversation, and so on? Do assessees seem to respond at all to the deeper and quicker suggestions for improvement they get from a peer assessor (as compared to a teacher)? Might this activity become self-sustaining without it having to be inflicted on the students?

Another issue is whether the peer assessment is aligned with the traditional forms of assessment. Will the peer assessment be taken into account when grading students at year end, for example, or does all of the assessment information for this have to be generated by the teacher? Do all students have to sit formal examinations irrespective? If so, is there any way you can use peer assessment to help them prepare for these examinations?

What transferable skills relevant to other activities might be measured as by-products of the process? Are you seeing improved social or communicative skills that might generalize beyond the peer assessment situation? Or writing skills or presentation skills? Or music skills or physical education skills? Might any of these endure beyond school? These are important by-products that should be taken into account when you are considering the success or otherwise of your peer assessment project.

Finally, is the peer assessment being evaluated, as one would hope with any new venture, or is its success or failure just assumed? Time spent evaluating is costly, and could be spent doing something else, but if you are to persuade the powers that be (within your school or wider than that) that peer assessment is worthwhile, you are going to need some evidence that looks at least a little bit objective.

Thus, it is clear that peer assessment is not just one method, but many. Labels can be given to some of these variations, distinguishing formative from summative peer assessment, qualitative from quantitative, structured from unstructured, unidirectional from reciprocal or mutual, same-year from cross-year, and same-ability from cross-ability peer assessment, for instance. These variations are summarized in Table 1.1 (below).

Table 1.1 Variations in Peer Assessment

	Alternative A	Alternative B	Comment
1	Summative	Formative	or both
2	Quantitative grading	Qualitative feedback	or both
3	Single product	Several products	
4	Same kind of product	Different products	
5	Same curriculum area	Different areas	
6	Assessment criteria clear	Not clear	
7	Students involved	Students not involved	in defining criteria
8	Rubric used	Rubric not used	
9	Training given to peers	Not given	
10	Feedback positive	Feedback negative	or both
11	Feedback→improvement	No improvement	
12	Product reworked	Not reworked	
13	Scaffolding given	Not given	prompts, cues, etc.
14	Individuals	Pairs	or groups
15	One-way	Reciprocal	or mutual in group
16	Matching deliberate	Matching random	or matching accidental
17	Matching academic	Matching social	or both
18	Same year of study	Different year of study	
19	Same class	Different class	
20	Same ability	Different ability	in this subject area
21	Previous experience	No previous experience	
22	Experience positive	Experience negative	or both
23	Cultural expectations positive	Negative	
24	Gender balance	Gender imbalance	ability, motivation, etc.?
25	Information technology	No IT	wholly or partly used?
26	In class	Out of class	or both
27	Length of sessions		
28	Number of sessions		
29	Objectives		Cognitive, metacognitive
30	Justification to peer	No justification	
31	Confidentiality	No confidentiality	to pair + teacher
32	Process monitored	Not monitored	

	Alternative A	Alternative B	Comment
33	Reliability moderated	Not moderated	and validity
34	Task simple	Or complex	or simple→complex
35	Feedback expected	Not expected	quantity + quality
36	Feedback objective	Feedback subjective	or both
37	Revisions many	Revisions few	
38	Intrinsic rewards	Extrinsic rewards	neither
39	Aligned	Non-aligned	with other assessment
40	Transferable skills	None measured	
41	Evaluated	Not evaluated	
42	Voluntary	Or compulsory	
43	Anonymous	Non-anonymous	

Using this table, teachers will be able to see what kind of peer assessment they intend to implement. Importantly, because all the variations are listed, teachers will not overlook any issue they should have considered. There are rather a large number of variables in the table, and some researchers have proposed clustering these. The difficulty is that different researchers propose different clusters, so I have left the list un-clustered.

Teachers can print this table off and simply circle their own choices for each variable that is relevant (maybe they will all be relevant). It is available on the accompanying website (www.routledge. com/9780815367659). The table can then be kept as a useful record.

What Is *Not* Peer Assessment?

"*Peer review*" is a term usually used in the professions with regard to anonymous peer review of a written submission (e.g. to a "peer reviewed" academic journal). It is occasionally used with reference to school children.

"*Peer feedback*" is a term much more commonly found with respect to school children. It refers to that part of peer assessment which involves peer assessors giving information to their assessees about how they found the strengths and weaknesses of the item that was assessed. However, this feedback can be marks or grades rather than elaborated verbal feedback, so it does not necessarily involve a two-way conversation. The feedback may or may not be given any justification. It is not necessarily reciprocal. It can be anonymous or online (e.g. Gielen et al., 2010).

"Self-assessment" is "an arrangement for learners and/or workers to consider and specify the level, value or quality of their own products or performances" (Topping, 2003: 58). In self-assessment, the intention is to engage learners as active participants in their own learning and foster learner reflection on their own learning processes, styles and outcomes. Consequently, self-assessment is often seen as a continuous longitudinal process that activates and integrates the learner's prior knowledge and reveals developmental pathways in learning. In the longer term, it might impact self-management or self-regulation of learning – facilitating continuous adaptation, modification and tuning of learning by the learner, rather than waiting for others to intervene. In this it is much the same as peer assessment. It is mostly found in college and university settings, and in studies of teachers assessing their own performance, at least so far as the reported literature is concerned.

The correlation between self-assessments and teacher assessments is very variable, ranging from 0.40 to 0.94 (Topping, 2003). This variation is undoubtedly a product of the amount of experience the self-assessor has, as well as age, subject, race and gender differences, among other things. Self-assessment has indeed been successfully undertaken with some rather unlikely populations in schools, including students with learning disabilities and pre-school and kindergarten children.

Fontana and Fernandes (1994) tested the effects of the regular use of self-assessment techniques on mathematical performance with children in 25 primary school classes. Children ($n = 354$) in these classes showed significant improvements in scores on a mathematics test, compared with a control group ($n = 313$). In a replication, Fernandes and Fontana (1996) found children trained in self-assessment showed significantly less dependence upon external sources of control and upon luck as explanations for school academic events, when compared to a matched control group. In addition, the experimental children showed significant improvements in mathematics scores relative to the control group.

Ninness, Ninness, Sherman and Schotta (1998) and Ninness, Ellis and Ninness (1999) trained school students in self-assessment by computer-interactive tutorials. Students received computer-displayed accuracy feedback plus reinforcement for correct self-assessments of their math performance. After withdrawal of reinforcement, self-assessment alone was found motivational, facilitating high rates and long durations of math performance.

McDonald and Boud (2003) trained high school students on their performance in external examinations. Ten high schools representative of the top, middle and bottom levels of academic achievement in national examinations were chosen and students trained in self-assessment by their normal class teachers as part of their final year curriculum. An experimental group comprising 256 participants received formal training in self-assessment skills for the entire three terms of the academic year. A control group was selected from matched classes not receiving such training. A significant difference favoring those trained in self-assessment was found overall and in each curriculum area.

Andrade, Du and Wang (2008) investigated the effect of reading a model written assignment, generating a list of criteria for the assignment, and self-assessing according to a rubric, as well as gender, time spent writing, prior rubric use, and previous achievement on elementary school students' scores for a written assignment ($n = 116$ grade 3 and 4 children). The comparison (alternative treatment) condition involved generating a list of criteria for an effective story or essay and reviewing first drafts. There was a main effect of experimental treatment and of previous achievement on total writing scores.

Thus, while the reliability and validity of teacher assessment is not high, that of self-assessment tends to be a little lower and more variable, with a tendency to over-estimation. The reliability and validity of self-assessment tends to be higher in relation to the ability of the learner, the amount of scaffolding, practice and feedback and the degree of advancement in the course, rather than chronological age. Other variables affecting reliability and validity include: the nature of the product or performance assessed, the nature and clarity of the assessment criteria, and the nature of assessment instrumentation.

Might we expect practice in self-assessment to improve the quality of peer assessment? Certainly. Might we expect experience of peer assessment to improve the quality of self-assessment? Without a doubt. Most teachers will favor peer assessment before self-assessment, on the grounds that children need experience of the wide world of variation in ability and performance before trying to place themselves in this variability without any benchmark.

If you want to read more about self-assessment, see the book in this series by Lois Harris and Gavin Brown (Harris & Brown, 2018).

Strengths

Peer assessment usually deals with the products of learning – often writing, but also oral presentations, portfolios, drawings, and so on – but also with other associated skilled behaviors – learning behavior or wider social behavior – and sometimes encompasses both academic products and associated behavior. Thus, peer assessment can not only consider the product of learning, but also the process behaviors which lead to learning.

During the process of peer assessment both assessor and assessee are presented with many intellectual challenges, set in the context of a piece of work that the assessee feels rather strongly about. As a result, both assessor and assessee have to think quite deeply, as well as negotiate a settlement, so not only are their thought processes stimulated, but their social skills as well. Consequently they both learn – and not just in one domain. So the investment of time by a teacher can reap rich rewards

There are immediate benefits of peer assessment for learning and achievement, but also longer term benefits with respect to transferable skills in communication and collaboration. There may also be ancillary benefits in terms of the self-regulation of the student's own learning. These benefits accrue to both assessors and assessees through the process of peer assessment. Peer assessment of learning and social behaviors sharpens and broadens the assessor's capabilities. Combining assessment of product and process can enhance student understanding of the consistency or mismatch between these, and different ways of learning beyond their own.

Once students are somewhat used to peer assessment and have overcome their initial fears and hesitations, reliability is likely to be quite high (indeed, not that different from teacher reliability) (Topping, 2003, 2009). Reliability can be increased by making model student work available to the assessors – a master version of correctness against which the work to be assessed can be compared. Additionally, assessors can be provided with scoring checklists or rubrics, to the design of which they have preferably contributed. Students need to know whether the peer assessments will be entered in any kind of high stakes assessment, such as end of year overall grades. Where this is the case, they will need to know what proportion of the total grade is determined by the teacher and what proportion by peer assessment.

Limitations

All teachers have too much to do and too little time to do it in. Lack of time is always the reason given for a failure to do anything new. The problem is that teachers want to keep doing everything that they have ever done while at the same time trying something new. This equation cannot be solved. Teachers have got to let something go in order to try a new development. Of course, they do not have to let it go forever. Just until they are clear whether the innovation is better, worse or the same as the old method.

Will peer assessment save time? Well, probably not when you are just figuring out how to implement it, and devoting time to training the children and monitoring their efforts. But later, when the children are experienced and peer assessment is running smoothly, you might save a good deal of time otherwise spent in massive amounts of assessment – especially of written products. It thus makes "continuous assessment" a very real and also very practical way of proceeding.

Another issue is who exactly is a "peer." Someone in the same class? Someone in the same year? Someone of the same ability in the subject in question irrespective of their chronological age? All of these are possible, except of course any member of staff is excluded and the "peers" all have the status of officially being learners. Equal status can be interpreted exactly (sometimes termed "near-peer") or with flexibility. In the latter case, a peer can be any student within a few years of schooling (far-peer).

Obviously, it is important that participating students are clear about the form and nature of peer assessment to be undertaken. Assessors may need to be given training in how to give positive, negative and neutral feedback, and maintain a balance between these. Equally, it is important that the recipient of feedback is ready to respond to it thoughtfully, deciding what points to accept and what not to accept, and using this selected information to either improve the existing piece of work (as in formative feedback) or future pieces of work (as in summative feedback).

Of course, a problem with peer assessment is that it may be less likely to be "correct" than teacher feedback. On the other hand, it is readily available in much larger quantity and more immediately than teacher feedback. Assessees just need to be somewhat cautious about peer feedback, and assessors cautioned that if they are uncertain they should not claim to be right, since they are not expected always to be right.

International Vocabulary

This book will be read all over the world. Different countries organize their education systems in different ways and use different vocabulary to describe them. Two kinds of confusion can arise: where different words are used for the same thing, and where the same words are used for different things. By way of example, some of the most common differences in vocabulary between the US and the UK are discussed below. I have tried to use the UK and US terms interchangeably in this book – so be prepared for some initial surprises.

Students/Pupils

In North America, learners in all kinds of schools and colleges and universities are often called "students." In the UK, the term "students" is only used for learners in colleges and universities, while learners in schools are termed "pupils" or "schoolchildren" or just "children."

Grade

In North America, grades are developmental levels of competence in school roughly corresponding to chronological years, but with the implication that children should meet the minimum level of competence for one grade before proceeding to the next (although this might not be enforced in practice). Grades are also found in other parts of the world. Most of the rest of the world groups children simply in chronological years, and all children progress with advancing age. Exceptions are in small (often rural) schools and in developing countries, which may have children from several years in one class. North American grade 1 (5–6-year-olds) roughly equates to English Year 1 (but in England there is an unlabeled year of school before that) and to Scottish P2 (Primary 2), and so on.

Types of School

In North America, "elementary" schools are for children aged approximately 5–11 years. These are called "primary" schools in the UK, and other things elsewhere in the world. Schools for children aged roughly 11–18 years are called "high" schools in North America, "secondary" schools in the UK, and other things elsewhere in the world. In some parts of both North America and the UK, "middle schools" will be found, taking children from about 9–10 years until 12–13 years.

Special Needs/Disability

Children with unusual or exceptional difficulties or needs in learning or coping with the school environment are termed children with "special educational needs" in the UK. In North America, the vernacular expression "special ed. students" is sometimes heard, but is often unacceptable to the students and their families. North America has an elaborate quasi-medical typology for labeling different kinds of difficulty in children (DSM-IV), but in the UK legislation largely prohibits such labeling and mandates a more specific and pragmatic focus on the special educational needs of the individual in relation to their current context. Teachers often ask whether peer assessment can be used with children with disabilities/special needs. The answer is almost always yes, although there may well have to be some initial special help by way of coaching from the teacher or classroom assistant.

Education Management

In the USA, education is a provincial and state responsibility, jealously guarded. Consequently, there is little national standardization of what schools have to teach, although there are some national assessments for older students. Sometimes individual States give curriculum guidelines, more or less prescriptively, which might relate to State-wide achievement tests where these are required. Within States, individual School Districts can also vary in the amount of curriculum prescription and mandated testing of outcomes.

In the UK, there is a prescribed and standardized "National Curriculum" with which all publicly funded schools must comply. There are also national tests at intervals throughout a student's school career, in addition to national examinations at the end of their time in school, and a national school inspection system. Local government is in the form of Councils or "local authorities," which previously used to allocate funds from central and local taxation to schools. However, this is increasingly channeled directly from central government, and the functions of local authority education departments considerably reduced.

Computers

In US schools, computer provision is typically relatively high, even some elementary schools having computer laboratories as well as many computers in classrooms. In the UK, although high schools might have computer laboratories, primary schools typically only have one or more computers in the classroom. Both countries suffer from an accumulation of elderly and ill-serviced hardware, and problems with training teachers and keeping them updated (particularly about software). UK schools have adopted the standard term "Information and Communications Technology" (ICT) to refer to this aspect of learning.

Why Read This Book?

This book focuses on how teachers can establish classroom contexts that support the use of effective peer assessment practices and design successful peer assessment activities – which work. The purpose of this book is straightforward – to give teachers information and guidance to fine tune their knowledge and ability to enable them to successfully implement peer assessment in their classrooms – firstly one type of peer assessment, then experiment with other kinds as their confidence grows.

This book is intended to make innovation and quality improvement easier, quicker and more assured for the busy professional who is striving to raise standards of achievement, improve school effectiveness, and develop collaborative community partnerships. The methods described are also enjoyable, and sociable and intrinsically rewarding – not only for the children but also for the teacher. They can help to create a co-operative and positive social ethos and promote social inclusion and citizenship.

The methods presented in this book should typically yield substantial measurable benefits in relation to their low cost of implementation. Of course, you will need to think about how well you have put peer assessment into practice. If you do half the program badly, you will not be successful – and that is true of anything. The quality of implementation is important.

Additionally, just because a method is effective does not ensure that it continues to be used. For example, some teachers can be heard to express declining interest in a particular method because it is not "the latest thing." Fortunately, most teachers are too sensible and pragmatic to be so easily influenced by concern with novelty. Indeed, amidst much talk of higher standards and targets, accountability and cost-effectiveness, governments around the world are showing greatly increased interest in evidence-based education and issues of school effectiveness.

How to Use This Book

This Introduction defines peer assessment and gives a typology exploring its different varieties. You will need to choose just one to start with! Then a second chapter presents a variety of examples of peer assessment, coupled with further case studies on peer assessment using information technology. Read the example closest to the age range you teach, and then read the others. You can learn something from each.

Chapter 3 is about organizing peer assessment, and this chapter is very important for you. It provides teachers with a plan or template to address as they work on designing their own peer assessment project. Chapter 4 summarizes the theory and evidence on peer assessment. You might find this rather heavy going and choose to leave it until later, when you have more time. Or you might take a look at the summary just now and then go back and read more later – perhaps just the primary or secondary sections if those are the areas in which you teach. Theory sounds rather dry and not very useful, but when you read it you will not find it as dry as you think.

Chapter 5 is about evaluation. I'm afraid you have to read this sooner rather than later if you hope to build in any evaluative components, since waiting until after the project is running is leaving it far too late. In these evidence-based times we are all expected to evaluate the success of innovations, so this suggests ways of doing this without spending too much time. Chapter 6 is about sustaining and embedding. You can leave this until after you have completed your first successful project. Finally, the learning journey readers have hopefully made so far is reviewed, and there is discussion of where they may wish to go next.

So, to start with, read the first three chapters in that order – that is: Introduction and Typology, Practical Case Studies, and Organization. See, that's less than half the book!

References

Andrade, H. L., Du, Y., & Wang, X. L. (2008). Putting rubrics to the test: The effect of a model, criteria generation, and rubric-referenced self-assessment on elementary school students' writing. *Educational Measurement, 27*(2), 3–13.

Fernandes, M., & Fontana, D. (1996). Changes in control beliefs in Portuguese primary school pupils as a consequence of the employment of self-assessment strategies. *British Journal of Educational Psychology, 66,* 301–313.

Fontana, D., & Fernandes, M. (1994). Improvements in mathematics performance as a consequence of self-assessment in Portuguese primary-school pupils. *British Journal of Educational Psychology, 64,* 407–417.

Gielen, S., Peeters, E., Dochy, F., Onghena, P., & Struyven, K. (2010). Improving the effectiveness of peer feedback for learning. *Learning and Instruction, 20*(4), 304–315.

Harris, L., & Brown, G. (2018). *Using self-assessment to improve student learning.* Routledge Student Assessment for Educators Series. (Ed. J. H. MacMillan). New York & London: Routledge.

McDonald, B., & Boud, D. (2003). The impact of self-assessment on achievement: The effects of self-assessment training on performance in external examinations. *Assessment in Education: Principles, Policy & Practice, 10*(2), 209–220.

Ninness, H. A. C., Ellis, J., & Ninness, S. K. (1999). Self-assessment as a learned reinforcer during computer interactive math performance – An experimental analysis. *Behavior Modification, 23*(3), 403–418.

Ninness, H. A. C., Ninness, S. K., Sherman, S., & Schotta, C. (1998). Augmenting computer-interactive self-assessment with and without feedback. *Psychological Record, 48*(4), 601–616.

Topping, K. J. (2003). Self and peer assessment in school and university: Reliability, validity and utility. In: M. S. R. Segers, F. J. R. C. Dochy, & E. C. Cascallar (Eds.), *Optimizing new modes of assessment: In search of qualities and standards.* Dordrecht: Kluwer Academic Publishers (also in Hebrew in Zohar, T. (2006). *Alternative assessment.* Raanana: Open University of Israel).

Topping, K. J. (2009). Peer assessment. *Theory into Practice, 48*(1), 20–27 (themed issue on classroom assessment). Also in K. Cauley & G. Panaozzo (Eds.) (2011). *Annual Editions: Educational Psychology 11/12.* London & New York: McGraw-Hill.

2

Peer Assessment in Practice

This chapter contains a section of practical examples of peer assessment in a variety of contexts in elementary school and in high school (and kindergarten as well!). Various activities and subjects are described. Then in a second section peer assessment using information technology is described in three case studies.

School Case Studies

We will start with an upper secondary context, then go to lower secondary, then to upper primary, then to lower primary, finishing with kindergarten. First, choose and read the example from the age range that you currently teach (even if you teach in a middle school). Then read the other examples.

Upper Secondary

An upper secondary school teacher in an English department wants to explore peer assessment of written analyses of a piece of Shakespeare. The hope is that this will engage the students more in what could otherwise become a mechanical exercise – writing only for the teacher. She is looking for more interactivity, better thinking, and greater generation of novel ideas. She discusses peer assessment with a colleague in her department, who is happy for her to take the initiative and will try it later in her own class if it works.

Knowing the students might balk at this new process, especially if it involves appearing unpleasant to their friends, the teacher takes care to introduce the idea gradually over a period of a few weeks. She divides the whole class into small groups to discuss the upcoming written task about Shakespeare. What might be the assessment criteria for this task? At first, the students are slow to respond, but eventually they warm up and generate a wide range of ideas about what a good essay would look like and what should be sought in the writing. The teacher works with them on synthesizing the criteria. Eventually, they have a reasonably short list of clear criteria. With one or two exceptions, the list is pretty much the same as the one the teacher herself would have used for assessing these papers, but the students do not know that.

The students are told that they will use these criteria to give feedback on each other's essays. They are divided into teams of three students of roughly similar ability in writing. This means that quite a few of the more able groups are all female and several of the less able groups are all male, but many in the middle are of mixed gender. The teacher takes care that each group contains no close friends (or enemies). Some students try to arrange to work with their friends, but the teacher tells them that would not be effective and is not part of the system.

The teacher then takes some time for training. She uses a similar, anonymous piece of writing done in the previous year. Displaying the piece together with the assessment criteria, she talks and shows by annotation how her mind is working as she makes assessment decisions about the manuscript, addressing each of the criteria. Then she invites the students to assess another previous year's paper in their groups, while discussing the task. They do this quite quickly. As she circulates, she can see that some groups manage very well, yet others need some encouragement or coaching, which she gives. The teacher sets them to work on the new task. Each student completes their essay, knowing that it will be peer assessed by both of the other members of the group. This sharpens their motivation to make a good job of it. They also know that they will need to peer assess two papers themselves.

The groups convene and students complete their peer assessments without discussion in the group, referring to the written assessment criteria and a short list of useful tips about peer assessment. They know that they have 40 minutes to complete the task of assessing two essays. As they work, the teacher goes round to look at what is being written and have a quiet word if anyone seems to be stuck. Most have finished within 30 minutes, and the teacher encourages them to make sure their assessments are all written down. She then lets them discuss the exercise until the end of the lesson, but not change their assessments. At the end of the lesson, each group hands in their written peer assessments to the teacher – six from each group of three people.

The teacher compares the two peer assessments for each essay. Where the two assessments are similar, she is content, and will pass both of these to the student who produced the work. Where they are very different, she notes that she will have to talk to this group next time they meet, and maybe even assess that essay herself before passing the assessments back to the student. Although there is sometimes a tendency for students' comments to verge towards the average (common with a first experience of peer assessment), she is aware that the next time the students will be more courageous. She is relieved that there is little sign of anyone giving a bad or good peer assessment just on the basis of personal preference.

At the next lesson, she gives the peer assessments back to the groups. An animated discussion ensues, not only about the nature of the comments on their analyses of Shakespeare but also about the merits and disadvantages of peer assessment. The students are a little dismayed that the teacher has not assessed the work herself but, on reflection, can see that their peer assessments are, by and large, just as useful in guiding revision. The class talks about how they might improve peer assessment the next time they do it.

Somebody suggests that they apply it to another upcoming task, giving group presentations. The teacher agrees, noting that she has expended time on the training and peer assessment sessions but saved considerable time in not having to provide feedback on all these pieces of work herself overnight.

In terms of saving a teacher's time (not an insignificant factor), you can see how while a teacher's time is saved in assessing her/himself, more time is expended in discussing and agreeing the assessment criteria, training the assessors in giving feedback, coaching while peer assessment is occurring, and so forth. So, in the short run, teacher time is not saved, but re-allocated to other activities. In the medium to long term however, as the teacher and the class become more used to peer assessment, there may well be some saving of teacher time. Moreover, there are likely to be benefits for teachers, as well as students. Peer assessment can lead teachers to scrutinize and clarify assessment objectives and purposes, criteria, and grading scales.

Lower Secondary

A lower secondary school teacher in a Social Studies department wants to explore peer assessment of individual presentations of individual project work and the effect on language development in children. The main audience for these presentations should thereby shift from the teacher (in assessment mode) to the peer group – which is of course where he wants the learning to be taking place. He is hoping for more debate and sharper identification of the key issues. He wants the students to really grapple with contentious concepts – which may hit some of them rather hard – and be prepared to stand up and defend their views, however conservative or radical. He discusses peer assessment with two colleagues, who are happy for him to take the lead and might try it later if it works.

He knows the students will not want to appear critical of their friends, but might be very happy to be critical of their enemies – and there may be other problems. So he introduces the idea gradually over a period. Individual presentations do, of course, have two aspects – one is the content and the other is the mode of presentation. Will this task cover only the first, only the second or both? After some thought, the teacher decides to peer assess only the mode of presentation. He realizes this will be conceptually challenging for his class, who are likely to first respond to content.

In a whole class discussion he raises the issue of the upcoming presentations – and says that there will be some peer assessment of mode of presentation. So, however much you agree or disagree with what the person is saying does not matter – what matters is how they are saying it. So what would be the characteristics of a good mode of presentation? What would you want it to do? The teacher divides the class into groups of four and encourages them corporately to develop a list of features of a well delivered presentation – and write them down. The students generate a wide range of ideas about what a good presentation would look, sound and feel like. Each group has part of the answer and the teacher synthesizes the criteria into a short list of clear criteria. With one or two exceptions, the list is pretty much the same as the one the teacher himself would have used for assessing these presentations, but the students do not know that.

The teacher then tells the students that they will use these criteria to give individual feedback on each other's presentations. However, as one peer assessment might be slightly askew or otherwise biased, each presentation will be peer assessed by two separate peers. Once they have assessed separately, the pair will come together to discuss and seek a jointly negotiated and agreed peer assessment.

Typically, in such situations the boys think they are better at it but actually they are not. So it makes sense to pair each presenter with a boy and a girl assessor. The assessors and the presenter should be of about the same level of ability. Each group should contain no close friends (or enemies). This does mean that the weaker presenters will also have the weaker assessors, but hopefully the weaker assessors will not be able to come up with such a long list of problem issues and thereby thoroughly depress the presenter.

The teacher then takes some time for training. He talks about the list of assessment criteria the group has generated. He shows a video of a similar presentation done in the previous year. He then addresses each item on the assessment list by discussion of how he feels the presentation met the criteria, allowing no interruption from the group. He is careful to start with positive points and only then go on to discuss things that could have been better. At the end, he allows comments from the group who might have agreed or disagreed with what he said – while pressing the respondent for reasons why they feel that way – in other words, on what evidence?

Then the teacher invites each member of the class to conduct an assessment of another video of an individual presentation from a previous year. First they are to do this individually, then after ten minutes they can discuss in their groups of four until they reach a consensus. As he circulates, the teacher can see that some groups manage very well, yet others need some encouragement or coaching, which he gives. The session concludes with a brief plenary where any differences in views are aired and the underpinning reasoning explored.

Over the next week, each student prepares their presentation. They know that it will be peer assessed by two other members of the group. This sharpens their motivation to make a good job of it. They also know that they will need to peer assess two presentations themselves.

The presentations are made and each pair of students completes their peer assessments without discussion on each one, referring to the written assessment criteria. They know that they have 40 minutes to complete the task of assessing two presentations. As they work, the teacher goes round to look at what is being written and have a quiet word if anyone seems to be stuck. The pairs are not in discussion at this stage. At the end of the lesson, each pair hands in their written peer assessments to the teacher – two from each person, four from each pair.

Over the next week the teacher compares the two peer assessments for each essay. Where the two assessments are similar, he is content, and will pass both of these to the student who produced the work. Where they are very different, he notes that he will have to talk to this pair at the next class meeting, and maybe even assess that presentation himself.

Although there is sometimes a tendency for students' comments to verge towards the average (common with a first experience of peer assessment), he is aware that the next time the students will be more courageous. There is little sign of anyone giving a bad or good peer assessment just on the basis of personal preference for the person.

At the next lesson, he gives the peer assessments back to the presenting student and to the assessing pair. The students are a little dismayed that the teacher has not assessed the work himself, but, on reflection, can see that their peer assessments are, by and large, just as useful in guiding improvements in their presentation style. An animated discussion ensues, not least about the merits and disadvantages of peer assessment. The class talks about how they might improve peer assessment the next time they do it. Somebody suggests that they apply it to another upcoming task. The teacher agrees, noting that he has expended time on the training and peer assessment sessions but saved considerable time in not having to provide feedback on all these pieces of work himself overnight.

Upper Primary

An upper primary school teacher has already done quite a lot of work on science. At the moment he is focusing on combustion, particularly the requirement for availability of oxygen in the air to allow combustion, as it is essentially a process of oxidation. He has conducted a whole class demonstration experiment on this topic and the children have written it up in individually their science notebooks, with appropriate diagrams. But now he is interested in whether the children can communicate what they are supposed to have learned – in other words, he is trying to stretch knowledge into communication of knowledge.

He divides the class into groups of four. Each group usually has two boys and two girls and a mixture of abilities. The task of each group is to prepare a poster that clearly shows this scientific idea – mainly in pictures. This poster is to be presented to the class with as much explanation as is felt necessary – except that all four group members must be involved in the presentation.

How will these posters and presentations be assessed – why, by peer assessment of course. Each poster presentation will be assessed by two other groups of four, who will have to discuss and negotiate an agreed joint assessment. This will be done anonymously – nobody will know who is conducting the peer assessment of whom. The two peer assessments then will be shown to the presenters (also anonymously) by the teacher. Where they are similar (and relatively positive) the assessors may be willing to be identified, in which case there can be a discussion between assessors and assessees. Where they are dissimilar, the teacher might need to intervene with some coaching about how to manage radically dissimilar views.

So what might be the peer assessment criteria? Are we trying to assess the content of the poster, or how it is presented, or both? The teacher decides to be ambitious and ask that the peer assessment covers both aspects. In a whole-class discussion he talks about these two aspects of presentations. He suggests one or two points under each heading that might be considered relevant, then asks for suggestions from the class. After a few minutes he lets the class divide into their groups of four, which he knows will let more voices be heard and give the lower ability children more chance to be heard. A plenary at the end enables him to make a short list of peer assessment criteria for both content and style of presentation.

The day of the presentations comes around and each member of each group has their own list of the assessment criteria (which, of course, they will have to use twice). They listen to the group presentations and (anonymously) make their assessments. They then need some time in a second lesson to gather as a group to negotiate a shared view on their individual assessments.

After the peer assessments have been given to the presenters and digested by them, a class plenary is held where the good and bad points of the exercise are discussed. Some students may not have liked it much but grudgingly agree that they have learned from it. Any suggestions for improving peer assessment can be heard. And there can be discussion of what peer assessment might be applied to next.

While teacher time is saved in assessing, more time is expended in discussing and agreeing the assessment criteria, coaching while peer assessment is occurring, and so forth. In the medium to long term however, as the teacher and the class become more used to peer assessment, there may well be some saving of teacher time.

Lower Primary

A lower primary physical education teacher is interested in football coaching. She is aware that much football coaching has involved putting the children on the field with a ball and hoping for the best, while the teacher is preoccupied with refereeing. She is hoping to do something that meets the individual needs of children rather better, and seeks improvement in very specific skills. She decides to focus on passing, with particular reference to length and direction, and consequently which part of the foot to use in what situation.

In a whole class presentation she outlines the issues of power and direction and consequently what part of the foot to use. She supports this by the use of diagrams, and even shows a video where these techniques are displayed. Now the children (at least those who were listening) should have the knowledge of how to pass with appropriate direction and control. But can they actually do it? More to the point, can they do it in the hurly-burly of a football match that involves a great many distractions?

In order to ascertain this we obviously need some form of individual assessment. What are the criteria for a successful pass? At short distance and at long? Adequate direction, adequate power? Correct use of the foot (left side foot, right side foot, frontal laces through it, backheel . . .)? And do we need to have this list twice, once in a quiet practice situation, and once in the course of a distracting match? The teacher suggests the first couple of criteria in each and then solicits more from the whole class. Eventually, a list of criteria in both settings is drawn up.

Now the difficulty is how to allocate time for peer assessment, since PE time is traditionally full of activity for all. Doing this only for passing and only in quiet practice time is one thing – it is easy enough to spend ten minutes while I observe you and then ten minutes while you observe me. But doing this in a football match is altogether different. The only way to do it is to have reciprocal peer assessment in pairs, with one person playing and the other assessing, and then the roles (and teams) switching at half time.

So this was what this teacher set out to do. She had the class divided into pairs, each pair of roughly equal ability in football (irrespective of gender). Each member of each pair had the list of assessment criteria. In the pre-match practice session, each pair took turns at assessing the others passing. In the actual match, in the first half one member of each pair would be assessing while one would be playing, and vice versa for the second half.

After the match the pair was given time to meet and compare their peer assessments. Areas of strength and weakness were identified (the areas of strength first, of course). Ideas were generated about how each player could improve their passing. Issues were brought to a whole-class meeting with the PE teacher, since many pairs turned out to have similar problems, and the teacher found ways of addressing at least some of them – as well as encouraging individuals to practice outside of school. Of course, there was a great deal of discussion in and out of school about all this – which was exactly what the teacher had hoped to achieve. Finding this successful, the teacher shared the idea with other colleagues who took children for PE – and encountered a good deal of interest. In terms of saving the teacher's time, the only extra task for the teacher was making copies of the list of assessment criteria, since the amount of time dedicated to PE was finite.

Kindergarten

Two kindergarten teachers who share the same large class want to be brave and explore peer assessment, although they are not sure it will work with such young children. They know language is really important for these children, but think that direct peer assessment of language would be too challenging especially as the girls tend to be better at language than the boys. So they think they will try peer assessment of drawing – at least that is an area where boys do as well as girls. And they think that during the course of peer assessment of drawing some interesting language will certainly be generated by the children.

The teachers also hope that peer assessment of drawing will help the children to think more clearly about what they are trying to achieve in their drawings. Although at this age drawing tends to be a very egocentric exercise, at a later stage drawings will become a means of communication, and perhaps the earlier children begin to realize this, the better.

But how to introduce this idea to the children? The teachers agree to take two examples of a drawing of a person done by students in a class from last year, one rather good and the other not very good. They gather the children round on the mat and show them these two pictures side by side (or via overhead projector or whiteboard if they are too small to see easily). They ask the children to consider the two pictures and decide which they would vote for as the best picture. After a few minutes those who like picture A best are asked to raise their hands. Then those who like picture B best (watching out for children raising their hands both times – or not at all.) Unsurprisingly, most children like the better picture best.

Now comes the interesting part. Why did most of you decide that this picture was the best? Who can tell me one thing you liked better in this picture, one reason why you chose this picture as the best? The children think and soon come up with suggestions (the teacher is careful the smart alecs don't monopolize the floor). On that one you can see a head. And two arms. And two legs. And the face has eyes. And a mouth. And a nose (maybe). And that one seems to be wearing clothes. And shoes (maybe). And that one has hands. Oh, and feet. And that one seems to be doing something, while the other one is not. One of the teachers is busy writing down these suggestions.

Once the children have finished (this isn't pushed to exhaustion) the teachers can show the list of features they have generated and illustrate each one, either on a poster, overhead projector or whiteboard. Then the children are thanked for responding so well and told they will come back to talk about this more tomorrow.

By the next day the teachers have made a copy of the list of features (with accompanying drawings) for every child in the class. Of course, for those children who can't yet read, the drawings are essential – but for everyone a list of words with accompanying drawings might do something for their sight vocabulary. Distributing these, they point out that the children have made a list of ways of telling whether one picture of a person is better than another. This will be very useful for the children to think about the next time they draw a picture of a person.

To help them with this thinking, the next time they draw a person they will be put into pairs. No, not in a pair with your best friend, because you already know how to get along with them. We will put you in a pair with someone you know but haven't had much to do with. That might be a boy or a girl. Then you will make a new friend. (What the teachers actually do is try to create pairs with some moderating social features, like putting a particularly impulsive boy with a particularly patient girl. Generally, the pairs should be of approximately the same overall ability. Yes, that means bright ones with bright ones and low ability students paired together. These latter will need more teacher help and might have poorer language, but at least will not feel that their picture is much worse than their partner's).

The teachers say that idea is that each of you will draw a person on your own. When you are finished, you will swap your picture with for that of your partner. Then your partner will look at her or his list of ways in which pictures can be better or worse, and see how many of these ways your picture shows. Remember that you have this list when you are drawing your picture, so you can remind yourself of what your partner is going to be looking for.

Then you get together and talk about what you have found out about each other's pictures. Of course, this is art work, so people are bound to have somewhat different feelings about pictures. Talk about sameness and difference in your feelings about each other's picture. Take care that first you say something about what your partner has done well. If you say something good to them they are more likely to say something good to you! Only later say anything about something you think they have missed out.

While this discussion is going on, both teachers are circulating and visiting with pairs to coach and support the conversations, and especially to help with any pairs who are finding it difficult. In this latter case, the teacher tries to model the appropriate behavior for the pair. The teachers are also in an excellent position to assess the level of language development being shown in the pairs.

After 10 to 15 minutes, the children are called to a halt (there will still be some who have a lot left to say . . .). Then in a whole-class discussion, the children are asked firstly, whether they liked that activity or not. Whatever the answer, individual children can be asked why they thought that. Then the children are asked whether they thought the activity was useful, in that they learned something from it (this is a rather different question, of course). Again, whatever they answer, they can be asked why. The children can also be asked if they would like to try this with a different kind of drawing, perhaps a drawing of a house. And would they like to stay with the same partner or perhaps change their partner? So at the end of each activity the seeds are sown which lead to the next peer assessment activity.

So what are the benefits for the teachers here? They have taken a modest amount of time to set up the activity. Some resources were required in terms of the sheet for each child, but not so many and that sheet will remain useful for the future. How much time have they saved in assessing the children's drawing themselves? Well, we could argue about whether teachers in kindergarten should be assessing children's drawings at all, but the fact remains that what has happened here is that all the children's drawing is likely to have been improved – a desirable educational goal. Additionally, a good deal more complex language has been generated among the children than normally occurs in free play. And the children have developed a peer assessment skill which can now be generalized to other situations.

Would you call this peer assessment when describing it to parents? Perhaps not, as that might alarm some of them. But describing it in simpler words and outlining the benefits it generates should go down well.

Peer Assessment through Technology

Generally, peer assessment through technology is much more frequent in colleges and universities than it is in schools, and more common in high schools than elementary schools. This may have something to do with the relative ease of access to computers in these places. It cannot be directly connected with class sizes, as elementary classes are as big as or bigger than those in high schools. It may also have something to do with the relative value placed on face-to-face contact in the different places. An edited book has been produced on *Self, Peer and Group Assessment* in e-learning (Roberts, 2006), and interested readers will find further detail here, although there is no representation from primary schools.

Technology can be used in various ways in relation to peer assessment:

1. The course itself might be delivered online – in which case online peer assessment follows relatively automatically.
2. Files containing the items to be assessed can be placed on a mutually accessible website or transferred by email, e.g. files from word processors, PowerPoint, web portfolios, Drawing and Painting programs, Excel, statistical packages, etc.
3. Tablets can also be used for one group to use cooperatively in the field, or for one group on a field trip to communicate with the rest of the team in the classroom, or for one team to be peer assessed by another team.
4. There are special programs for matching students for peer assessment. This can be done randomly or according to various criteria such as previous ability or gender.
5. Technology can provide means of communicating about peer assessment, via "ordinary" tools such as email, Facebook, Twitter, Skype, etc. or by special tools within a VLE (virtual learning environment) or MOOC (Massive Online Open Course). The communication can be synchronous (both people present at the same time) or asynchronous (people only present at different times – obviously this is slower). The online communication can be for people who know each other and therefore be supplemented by face-to-face interaction in real time, in which case the communication could be described as "blended." Or it might be between people who have never met other than online – or between

people who remain anonymous and indeed might be separated by thousands of miles!

6. Technology can provide a means of recording the peer assessments and summarizing or analyzing them, especially when they are grades rather than qualitatively elaborated. For example, Tseng and Tsai (2007) found different kinds of feedback more or less effective at different times. Lu and Law (2012) investigated the effectiveness of feedback that identified problems and suggested solutions.

7. Lastly, technology can offer a means of assessment through analysis of artifacts captured within it, e.g., via capture of emails back and forth, by real time video taken of face-to-face interactions by Skype, by online questionnaires, screen capture, and so forth.

Now let us look at some reports of peer assessment using technology.

An Online Course

Tseng and Tsai (2007) studied the effects and validity of online peer assessment in high schools. In an online computer course the students (184 tenth graders) developed their individual course projects and then conducted online peer assessment. Each student acted as an assessor for one other student's project and as an assessee for their own project. However, the scoring criteria were devised by the teachers rather than a product of involvement by the students. There were three rounds of peer assessment. The students significantly improved their projects as a result of involvement in the peer assessment activities.

The study also examined the relationship between types of peer feedback and their subsequent performance in their projects. Reinforcing peer feedback (in which peer assessors said which parts of the project were the best) was useful in helping students' development of better projects. However, an excess of Didactic feedback (students behaving too much like teachers!) was not helpful. Suggestive feedback was helpful in the beginning of peer assessment activities but not so significant later.

Thus this study involved aspects 1, 2, 5 and 6 from the list of ways of using technology given above. See if you can figure out how many ways of using technology featured in the next two studies.

An Online Learning Platform

Lu and Law (2012) pointed out that online peer assessment has several advantages over face-to-face assessment. For instance, it allows anonymous marking and feedback, which can facilitate a willingness in students to critique the work of peers. It makes it easier for teachers to monitor students' online participation and progress. Online assessment systems can also provide teachers and researchers with valuable information about student online assessment behavior and performance because they can automatically record data about student assignments, participation and communication. Online assessment systems are more flexible because they allow students to assess the work of peers outside of fixed class schedules. Finally, online assessment systems can automatically assign students to review more heterogeneous or homogeneous work based on such background features as gender, achievement and preferences.

However, they neglected to mention any disadvantages of online peer assessment, such as how it is generally very difficult for online response to embody the non-verbal components of affective feedback – in other words, the assessor cannot get over their feelings about the work to nearly the same extent, nor can they see how pleased or upset the assessee is in response.

Lu and Law (2012) note that online peer assessment systems can provide such functions as assignment submission, storage, communication, and review management. They mention the "NetPeas" system, a web-based peer assessment system that allows assignment modification and uploading, peer assessment, and complaint filing. They also mention the "Group Support System," which provides such functions as discussing assessment criteria and collaborative assessment.

The authors studied 181 13–14-year-old lower secondary students in a medium social economic status public school in

Hong Kong. The students belonged to five different classes and were taught Liberal Studies by five different teachers. The students worked on a six-week project using an online learning platform called Interactive Learning and Assessment Platform (iLAP). This poses many challenges to high school teachers and students in Hong Kong because it adopts an inquiry-based learning approach. It was developed to help teachers manage, support, and assess learning, including processes and inquiry outcomes. iLap support includes: (1) assignment submission, (2) rubric development, (3) assessment implementation, and (4) performance monitoring. Students can upload assignments to the platform. iLAP enables teachers to create rubrics by specifying criteria for rating task dimensions and varying levels of performance. iLAP also supports self-assessment and teacher assessment as well as peer assessment.

Students were divided into small (n = 4–5) groups and submitted assignments online for review and comment by fellow group members. The peer assessment interface had two parts: a rubric area and a comment area. When an assignment was selected, the rubric assigned by the teacher was loaded and shown to assessors. The rubric had five criteria: (1) topic researchability, (2) clarity, (3) relevance and background information, (4) methodology, and (5) writing. Each criterion was further divided into four levels of quality: cannot be assessed (score 0), needs improvement (score 1–3), satisfactory (score 4–6), and excellent (score 7–9). Students clicked on drop-down menus to choose level of quality for each category. iLAP automatically calculated total scores. Students commented on assignments in the comment area. Teachers had access to clear summaries of assignment submissions and assessments of student performance. Student work was listed with peer assessment information including grades and comments.

Study participants did projects based on one of three topics: Consumer Education, City Transportation and Development, and City Economy. Their teachers divided the projects into five subtasks: (1) collect three topic relevant photos and formulate a research question, (2) draft project plans for investigating the research question, (3) prepare interview questions and identify possible interviewees, (4) draft questionnaires for the investigation, and (5) write up project reports. The teachers gave the students rubrics for evaluating the work of peers on each subtask. Although students were encouraged to engage in peer assessment for all sub-tasks so as to become involved in a continuous process of reflection and improvement, students could choose which subtask(s) to assess. Students first graded the work of peers based on rubrics and then made optional comments. Grades and comments were immediately available to assessees through iLAP.

Peer feedback was qualitatively analyzed using a coding schema based on relevant literature. Comments were first coded as affective and/or cognitive. Affective comments were further categorized as positive (e.g. "Very good") or negative (e.g. "badly written"). Cognitive comments were categorized as (1) identifying the problem; (2) a suggestion; (3) an explanation; and (4) a comment on language. Data from the five classes were collapsed for analysis because: (1) students from the five classes did not differ in their academic performance in general; (2) teachers taught the five LS classes in rotation to assure equivalence among the classes. The materials and tasks on iLAP were consistent for all five classes; (3) the five classes did not differ in final project scores and (4) multilevel intraclass correlation on class dependence was 0.01 indicating no variance difference among the five classes.

Science Web Portfolios

Yes, that one was more complex, wasn't it? Now let's try another complex one. Hovardas, Tsivitanidou, and Zahcharias (2014) involved secondary school students in reciprocal peer assessment. Randomly matched participants worked in groups of two to create web portfolios; group composition did not change during the intervention. All students had prior experience with recipro-cal peer assessment of web portfolios. They served as individual assessors during the first phase of producing peer feedback, while they formed pairs (assessee groups of two students) at the subse-quent phase of review of peer feedback. Pre-specified assessment criteria were used to rate science web-portfolios (i.e. a kind of quantitative peer feedback), and students were interviewed to ensure they understood the assessment criteria. Participants were then asked for written comments justifying their ratings and to suggest possible changes for revision (qualitative peer feedback).

Students worked with "Stochasmos," a web-based learning platform that supports collaborative learning in an inquiry based environment. It was chosen because the participants were already familiar with it and it had the features (e.g., web-portfolio, synchronous communication through a chat tool) necessary for the purpose of this study. In particular, the students studied material on CO_2 friendly houses, namely, houses made with specific modifications during the building and operation phases in order to produce lower CO_2 emissions than conventional houses. This learning material required students to create a number of learner products (e.g., concept maps, tables, text), which were included in the students' web-portfolios.

Students first watched a video and identified the most important information it presented concerning renewable sources of energy, and then stated a hypothesis concerning the central question of the activity sequence ("If all homes in the country used solar energy by setting up solar cells, to what degree would we reduce our carbon footprint?"). In the second step students studied relevant texts and then wrote a report presenting what they had identified as the most important information concerning the climatic conditions in the country.

In the third step, students carried out a Web Quest investigation that involved finding information on the ecological (web-based material on greenhouse effect, climate change, the Kyoto protocol, and actions that can be taken to face the problem of climate change), architectural (web-based material on bioclimatic architecture and real eco-houses), energy-related (web-based material on renewable sources of energy and ways to save energy), and insulation-related (web-based material on insulation for buildings/materials and different modes of insulation) aspects of a CO_2-friendly house. In the fourth step students studied material on the operation of a power station, as well as on hydroelectric energy, wind energy, and solar energy, and wrote short reports.

The final step was for students to address the central question, as well as to explain the reasoning behind the methods they followed while compiling the information needed for answering the central question. In total, it took the student groups in the study about ten hours to complete this activity sequence.

All web-portfolios should have thus included nine learner products: (1) a report on renewable energy; (2) the hypothesis concerning carbon footprint reduction; (3) a report on the climatic conditions in the country; (4) a report about the operation of a power station; (5) a report on water energy, (6) a report on wind energy; (7) a report on solar energy; (8) a presentation of the methodology followed while compiling the information needed for answering the central question; and (9) a final report with an answer to the central question.

A reciprocal peer assessment approach was used in an anonymous format. Participants worked in groups of two (home group) while developing learner products. However, they carried out the role of peer assessor on an individual basis, which allowed the production of two separate sets of peer feedback for each home group. After all students completed all tasks, peer assessors could access the web-portfolio of the peer group they were to assess, which was randomly assigned to them. Each web-portfolio was assessed by two peers from the same home group, who worked on different computers.

This procedure resulted in a list of 36 assessment criteria grouped into three main categories: (1) content of web-portfolios, (2) student skills, as displayed in web-portfolios, and (3) appearance and organization of web-portfolios. Assessors rated student performance on all criteria according to a three-point Likert scale (1 = unsatisfactory; 2 = moderately satisfactory; 3 = fully satisfactory). Assessors were also instructed to provide written feedback (for each criterion separately), in which they were to explain the reasoning behind their ratings, provide judgments and suggestions for revisions. On average, it took each peer assessor about an hour to complete the assessment.

After all peer feedback was submitted, the system sent feedback from two peer assessors to the corresponding assessee group. They were then allowed time to review the peer feedback and make revisions, which in most cases did not take more than an hour. Peer assessees were instructed to use peer and expert feedback to improve their web-portfolios but were not required to follow strictly or take as obligatory any suggestion or recommendation. Assessed groups had the opportunity to request elaboration concerning any of the peer criticisms through the communication/chat tool available in Stochasmos.

The data collection process involved: (1) peer feedback, (2) screen captured and videotaped data, and (3) peer assessee responses to peer and expert feedback received (through the questionnaire). The peer assessment data was stored along with the corresponding log files (accessible only by the teachers), which included information necessary for analysis, such as the name of the peer assessor, the date and time the feedback was created, revised, revisited, etc.

Screen captured data were collected with relevant software (River Past Screen Recorder Pro). This allowed the collection of a rich record of actual computer work activity in its natural work setting, showing the users' movement among various parts of the web-based material. The software also allowed videotaping of the students in conjunction with what was taking place on the screen.

The quantitative feedback was found to differ between peer assessors assessing the same web-portfolio. However, qualitative feedback was similar in its structural components. The majority of changes proposed by peer assessors were scientifically accurate and assessee groups employed decision-making strategies to screen and process peer feedback.

What Will You Do?

If you are interested in technology, you might want develop a peer assessment project that uses it. But remember that the technology should actually add value, either in terms of making complex processes simpler and quicker (for assessors, assessees or teachers, or all of these), or alternatively enabling something to be done which was not possible with pencil and paper or face-to-face conversation, or both of these.

Going on from case studies of peer assessment in action, the next chapter is very important – it tells you how to organize your own first peer assessment project.

References

Hovardas, T., Tsivitanidou, O. E., & Zahcharias, C. Z. (2014). Peer versus expert feedback: An investigation of the quality' of peer feedback among secondary school students. *Computers & Education*, *71*, 133–152.

Lu, J., & Law, N. (2012). Online peer assessment: Effects of cognitive and affective feedback. *Instructional Science*, *40*(2), 257–275. DOI: 10.1007/s11251-011-9177-2.

Roberts, T. S. (2006). *Self, peer and group assessment in e-learning.* Hershey, PA: Information Science Publishing.

Tseng, S. C., & Tsai, C. C. (2007). On-line peer assessment and the role of the peer feedback: A study of high school computer course. *Computers and Education*, *49*(4), 1161–1174.

3

Organizing Peer Assessment

There is no doubt that peer assessment can work. That is unequi
vocally demonstrated by the research evidence. However, the
evidence also shows that peer assessment can fail to work,
and failure you cannot afford. Careful planning is necessary to
ensure that you are successful. This is particularly important if
the project is a first venture.

This chapter on organization forms the core of this book. It is
long, but divided into 12 sections that relate exactly to the sections of the Organization Template in Table 3.2, which will be
found at the end of this chapter:

A. Context
B. Objectives
C. Curriculum Area
D. Participants
E. Helping Technique
F. Contact

G. Materials
H. Training
I. Process Monitoring
J. Assessment of Students
K. Evaluation
L. Feedback

To enable you to print out this table, you can find it at www.routledge.com/9780815367659.

After reading this chapter on organization (some sections maybe more than once), you should be in good shape to start planning your own peer assessment project, using a printed copy of the template to frame and record your planning decisions.

Of course, you will find some questions or pointers blindingly obvious, so forgive me for being over-inclusive. However, different people might find different points obvious.

A. Context

All children are different, and classes and schools are even more different from each other. All successful peer assessment projects have certain common elements, but each must be designed to fit comfortably within the ecology of a particular school at a particular time in its development.

Schools

What kind of school do you work in? Kindergarten (nursery), elementary (primary) school, middle school, high (secondary) school, or special school? Different kinds of school have different pedagogical styles, materials and methods, teacher responsibilities, organizational structures, and chains of command.

Problems

Careful consideration should be given to potential problems that are specific to your individual establishment. There may be difficulties with problems in a particular curriculum area in a particular age group, or with a large proportion of ethnic minority pupils struggling to learn the majority language, or with a high proportion of students with special needs. The peer group may be divided into sub-groups, with poor relationships between them, and there may be a high incidence of behavior problems in the classroom setting.

The facilities, resources and curriculum in the school may be outdated or poorly organized or culturally inappropriate. It is very important that peer assessment projects are not used to compensate for, and thereby perhaps disguise, fundamental weaknesses in the professional teaching or organizational infrastructure within a school. Schools that have failed to organize many things are unlikely to have any greater success with peer assessment.

However, do not despair. Peer assessment is not a fragile methodology that only works in ideal situations where there are no problems. It can be used carefully to address some of these problems. Indeed, in some cases it takes what you thought was a problem and turns it into an opportunity.

Support

Although it is possible to operate a peer assessment project in isolation within the confines of your own classroom, some support from colleagues inside or outside the school is highly desirable. At the very least, the agreement of the school principal will be essential. If this is a new venture for the school, advice and support from colleagues in other, more experienced, local schools or specialist advisory agencies should be sought.

Your professional colleagues may either: (a) go out of their way to express disapproval or be more tangibly obstructive; (b) be indifferent; (c) express positive attitudes and give you encouragement, but not actually do anything to help; or (d) be very interested and prepared to offer you practical help, time and resources, perhaps as part of a learning exercise for themselves.

Be very clear about the delegation of any tasks relevant to your project. You are likely to find it useful to complete the Organization Template (Table 3.2) and circulate copies of it to colleagues who are supporting you, so they are fully aware of the organizational structure of the project – and you may care to indicate their responsibilities with a highlighter.

B. Objectives

A clear and focused sense of objectives and purpose will guide your onward planning, and help prevent you from becoming muddled or over-complicated, and from taking on too much work. Also, clear objectives give a framework for eventual evaluation of the project.

Be clear about how your intentions align with the existing curriculum and existing instructional goals and objectives. A peer assessment project should not be a bolt-on appendage (risking looking like a transient whim or purely a search for novelty) – it should be integrated with overall pedagogical aims for the year.

Are you aiming for formative or summative assessment? Formative assessment is much safer for a first project and avoids much potential controversy. You might, of course, argue for it being formative assessment initially, but eventually contributing to summative assessment in some way in the future.

Can you make any argument for teacher time saving? Be careful here, as while you can argue that peer assessment will save teacher time in the medium to long term, you cannot argue that it will save time immediately, as in the short term you will be preoccupied with planning and preparation, training and monitoring.

Are you aiming for gains in achievement ('academic' attainment or 'cognitive' gains)? Or 'meta-cognitive' gains, so that students show more insight into their own learning processes and thereby become better able to regulate and control them productively? Or motivational gains, so students try harder and appear to value learning more? Or attitudinal gains, in terms of improved attitudes to the curriculum area, or improved attitudes to each other, or improved attitudes towards themselves (in terms of gains in self-esteem and self-confidence and higher expectations)? Or social and behavioral gains, with students becoming more collaborative and less competitive, more on-task and in-seat, more able to work in teams, more able to give and receive praise, more nurturing and less hostile, more cohesive and less alienated?

Which of these are you targeting for the assessees? Which of these are you targeting for the assessors?

How might these changes be measured? If your objectives are framed only in very vague general terms (e.g. "improved classroom atmosphere"), how will you know if they have or have not been achieved? What exactly would you expect to see and hear which would be good evidence that the "classroom atmosphere" had indeed "improved"?

Objectives do need to be realistic. Do not be over-ambitious, or you will just build in failure for yourself. It might be reasonable to expect both helpers and helped to show increased competence in the curriculum area, and perhaps increased confidence and interest in that area. A degree of reasonable caution when setting objectives creates the possibility of subsequently being pleasantly surprised.

Also remember that your objectives might well be quite different from the (unspoken) objectives of the students. They might just be seeking entertainment, in which case you had better make sure that your peer assessment program is enjoyable for the students, until deeper and more intrinsic motivation kicks in. Sometimes students have quite bizarre ideas about what peer assessment might be, which can interfere in a troublesome way until these ideas are unlearned, so take the time to explore existing pre-conceptions and resistances with your students. Student acceptance and ownership is likely to be better if students perceive that peer assessment has been introduced for developmental rather than administrative purposes, and detailed feedback is not directly accessed by authority figures.

C. Curriculum Area

What products will be assessed? For example:

- Writing
- Drawing
- Oral statements

- Presentations
- Portfolios
- Movement
- Performance
- Other?

Please be specific when you define the products. Will there be single or multiple assessments of each product (i.e. by one assessor or two or more)?

Although peer assessment can include peer oversight of punctuation, capitalization and grammar in the context of continuous writing, an excess of emphasis on such mechanical aspects of the writing process is likely to be joyless and risk neglecting the main purpose of writing. Once students are competent at peer assessment on single items of writing, their attention could productively turn to larger targets, such as whole collections or portfolios of written work.

Many teachers allow and encourage students to "help each other at the computer," but rarely have a clear and systematic procedure for this that maximizes effective learning and guarantees gains for both helper and helped. Unless the class teacher has a particular interest or is particularly capable, some of the students are likely to be more skillful than the teacher in this area. Peer assessment principles enable the design of effective means of utilizing the great potential of peers in this area.

Peer assessment during class time does, of course, have an opportunity cost – while you are doing peer assessment you are not doing something else. You should tackle this 'curriculum displacement' issue head on, since if you try to do peer assessment as an 'extra' while still doing everything else as well, you will go crazy and probably end up doing nothing properly.

However, peer assessment often adds extra value, in that it impacts on more than one curriculum area simultaneously. For example, a peer assessment program might have attainment effects and also social effects, related to both the regular subject area and to the personal and social development or citizenship curriculum. Two interventions for the price (and time) of one!

D. Participants

Think about arrangements to introduce peer assessment to students gently. Longer and longer mentions over a period of weeks will be better than dropping it all on them in one day. Will some of your students be resistant to the idea? Is this likely to be the very able and the least able – for different reasons? In your discussions with the students you had better be sure that you have your arguments well marshaled. Will there be resistances from students with a cultural heritage that finds peer assessment unusual?

Is there a degree of trust and psychological safety among the students – or just some of the students with some other students? What about the previous experience of the students? Have they done anything before, perhaps in another class, that might prepare them for peer assessment? Some peer tutoring or cooperative learning, perhaps? Might they have some pre-existing relevant skills? Do you think their previous experience was positive or negative? Do the students have any grasp of the idea of interdependence, and expect it in the process of peer assessment? Importantly, will you make peer assessment compulsory for all, or will you allow it to be voluntary (perhaps for a smaller group) at the outset? If you anticipate major student resistance, you might be best advised to make it voluntary initially.

What will be the nature of your matching process? If you know the students well, you might aim for matching pairs on the basis of ability. Will you want to pair students of similar ability? Or will you want triads with one student high ability, one medium and one low? Or some other arrangement?

However, you might not know the students that well, or you might not be aware of their relative abilities in the area in which you hope to do peer assessment. In this latter case, you might go for random matching – put all their names in a hat and have the students draw them out at random. Be careful about making your matching accidental, since it is likely that peer friendships will creep in, and you do not want friends partnered with friends.

Contact

Assessors – do we mean individuals, pairs or groups (and if groups, of what size?)? Assessees likewise – do we mean individuals, pairs or groups (of what size?)? Will the peer assessments be confidential or public? Will the peer assessment partner(s) be anonymous to each other or will they be known to each other?

Is a cross-institution or cross-building program desirable or feasible, or would the difficulties of synchronizing time-tables and arranging and supervising transport or movement from place to place be just too much? If the helpers are older, mature, and reliable, the latter might not present too much difficulty – but particularly for a first project, you should try to minimize the things which can go wrong.

Even within the same building, peer assessment between two different classes (whether of the same or different ages/grade levels) can present problems if the class rooms are far apart, or the route between them is complex or replete with other attractions. For a first experiment, peer assessment within one class over which the innovating teacher has total control certainly has advantages – less to go wrong and no one else to blame if something does.

Consideration is also needed of whether the peer assessment will be class-wide on an equal opportunity basis, or whether it will be confined to a selected sub-group. Teachers who are somewhat anxious about launching into a class-wide approach might prefer to start with a selected sub-group, but this should be representative of the whole class rather than some elite.

However, you should take great care that you do not give signals that peer assessment can only be done by particular types of student – especially not **only** by those students who are most like the teacher. Also be careful about signals regarding who it is done **to**, or stigmatization will result. It is as well to publicly rationalize starting with a sub-group as a trial or pilot, which will be extended to all students if it proves to be a success.

Class-wide peer assessment is almost always compulsory, although students typically do not notice its compulsory nature, accepting it naturally as another class activity. You might feel that asking for volunteers would ensure well-motivated participants and maximize your chances of success. While this is true up to a point, you need to consider the nature of the volunteer helpers – if they are predominantly white middle-class females, the sociological implications of deploying them with ethnic minority socio-economically disadvantaged males needs to be thought through. By sending out the wrong social signals, you might actually reduce the already limited inclination to participate of some students even further. You want peer assessment to be seen as enjoyable, desirable, and 'cool' by all your students.

Background Factors

All teachers have experienced the great variations in general maturity levels shown by classes in different years. In cases of uncertainty it is usually wisest to start with a small pilot project, to enable further helpers to be added to the project subsequently as a "privilege." Where the children have already been used to taking a degree of responsibility for independently guiding their own learning and/or working on co-operative projects in small groups, they may be expected to take to peer assessment more readily. You will need to consider these issues for both helpers and helped.

Having said that, peer assessment can improve peer group relationships, serve to develop social cohesiveness, and improve work habits. Thus some teachers deliberately deploy it in situations where there is a widespread lack of sharing, co-operation and mutual understanding in a group of children. However, more ambitious operations of this sort are perhaps best left to the more experienced.

Age

Organizationally, students of the same age, grade or year are usually easier to bring together. If you intend to use helpers who are considerably older than the helped, unless you are fortunate enough to teach a vertically grouped or mixed-age class, you are likely to find the organization of the project considerably more complicated, particularly if the helpers are to be 'imported' from another school. However, the novelty and nurturing effect of working with older pupils does add an additional effect.

Gender

Your class might not have evenly balanced genders. In any case, the girls are likely to be generally more socially responsible than the boys. So (leaving aside any other criterion for the moment), would you want mostly same-sex or mostly opposite sex pairings? Research suggests that male–male pairings tend to be successful, but female–female not so much, which leaves you with a surplus female problem if you opt for the former. You do need to be careful that you do not have too many girls in role as assessors, since this may generate umbrage among the boys – particularly those who are inclined to the view that females are inferior and should not be in positions of power. However, one effect of cross-gender helping may be to improve relationships and dispel stereotypes.

Numbers of Participants

Figure out your target totals of helpers and helped. It is always as well to start with a small number of children in the first instance. Resist any temptation to include "just one more," or before you know where you are the whole thing will become unmanageable. Particularly for a first venture, it is important to be able to monitor closely a modest number of children, and do everything well. At this stage do not worry about those who have to be "excluded," provided it is a representative sample of all your students rather than a particular type of student that is socially excluded. They can have a turn later, or be incorporated into the project as your organization of it becomes more fluent, automatic and confident. Besides, if any evaluation is to be carried out, it will be useful also to check the progress of a comparison group of children who have not (for the time being) been involved in the peer assessment.

Contact Constellation

Most peer assessment is done in a one-to-one situation, but it can occur in small groups of three, four or five children. Will the peer assessment be one-way or reciprocal? Or will each assessor have their work assessed by a different peer? It is also possible to have two helpers working with a small group of several assessees, but this is more complex and really best done with students already quite sophisticated in peer assessment methods.

For peer assessment, the assessor and assessed student do not necessarily need to be in contact for the actual assessment, but they do need to be in contact to give the assessment feedback and discuss it. If they are not in contact during the assessment, the assessor will obviously need to make some notes or fill out an assessment schedule or rubric in preparation for the ensuing discussion.

If you choose small groups, it is important to make the rules for the group and the specific roles of helpers and helped very clear, or the children may spend more time arguing about organization than actually getting on with the task in hand. You might also find that a small group encourages some students to be "passengers." It is much more difficult to become disengaged in a pair.

Ability

The range of ability in the children is a critical factor in selection and matching of helpers and helped. When drafting an initial matching on the basis of ability, the names of the available children should be ranked by the teacher in terms of their attainment in the curriculum area of helping. This can be done on the basis of teacher knowledge of the students in the class room situation, or on the basis of recent test results, or on a combination of these, or on any other indicators which the teacher deems reasonably reliable and relevant.

For a same-ability project (usually within one class, and often involving reciprocal helping), in the one ranked list pair the most able helper at the top of the list with the next most able student who is immediately next on the list, and so on.

For a cross-ability project within one class, in the one ranked list draw a line through the middle of the list separating helpers at the top from the helped at the bottom, and then pair the most able helper with the most able helped, and so on.

For a cross-ability peer assessment project between an older and younger class, in which all the older students were helpers and all the younger students were helped, the teachers would produce a ranked list for each class, then pair the top helper with the top student to be helped, and so on down the list. A widely used rule of thumb is to try to keep a differential of not more than two years in attainment between all helpers and helped in such a project – otherwise the helpers will get bored.

Reciprocal peer assessment is usually done with same-ability pairs, but not always. Some programs deliberately include a component requiring the weaker partner in a cross-ability pair to attempt to help the more able partner (even though the more able partner is unlikely to need it or benefit directly), so that the weaker partner can benefit from the cognitive challenge of helping and it does not all seem one-sided. Other programs have the partners helping each other in somewhat different areas, one partner being strong and a good helper in one area, the other being strong and a good helper in another area. This is often done when working with students with special needs as well as special strengths, i.e. an uneven profile of skills. Areas of relative competence and strength can be identified with all students, even those with many special needs.

Of course, there can be difficulties if the range of ability in helpers and helped is not evenly in parallel, perhaps if an older class of helpers is exceptionally able and those to be helped are a particularly poor "year," or if the spread of attainment in one group is very wide or very narrow or very uneven. Do not worry too much – just match them up as best you can and see what happens – this is not an exact science. Just try to maintain a helper/helped differential that is neither too big nor too small, to maximize the likelihood of gains for both helpers and helped.

Arranging same-ability pair matching with reciprocal peer assessment is perhaps the most common. This implies matching students with peer assessors they are likely to find credible. Cross-ability matching is less likely to be reciprocal, as the weaker partner would probably have difficulty appreciating the subtleties of the more able partner's work.

Relationships

The student's ability is the most important, but by no means the only, factor which must be taken into account. Pre-existing social relationships in the peer group must also be considered. Obviously, it would be undesirable to pair a child with another child with whom there is a pre-existing very poor relationship. However, do not adapt very many of the draft matched pairings on this basis, since part of the value of peer assessment is to give students a secure framework within which to relate productively. They do not need to learn to relate to peers to whom they can already relate, they need to learn to relate to students with whom they cannot readily relate.

On the other side of the coin, to pair children with their "best friends" of the moment is unlikely to be a good idea, particularly as the friendship may be of short duration. When children ask "can I work with my friend?, they often mean "can I not-work with my friend?" Especial care is necessary with the pairings in cases where the helped students are known to be of a particularly timorous or over-dependent personality, or helpers are known to be rather dominant or authoritarian by nature. You can also find this the other way round.

Participant Partner Preference

You might think it desirable to take the individual preferences of the participants themselves into account in some way, and some children might surprise you with the maturity they show in selecting a helper they think would be effective in this role. However, note the point made above about learning to make new relationships. Also consider that to allow completely free student selection of helper is likely to generate a degree of chaos, not least because some helpers will be over-chosen, while others may not be chosen at all, quite apart from the question of maintaining the requisite differential in ability. Many of these social considerations apply equally to the establishment of pairings of mixed race. Peer assessment can offer a focus for social contact between children who might otherwise be inclined to avoid each other owing to completely unfounded assumptions or anxieties.

Standby Helpers

It is always worthwhile to nominate a "supply" or "stand-by" helper or two, to ensure that any absence from school of the usual personnel can be covered. Children acting as spare assessors need to be particularly stable, sociable and competent, since they will have to work with a wide range of students to be helped. However, do not worry about imposing a burden on the spare helpers, as they may be expected to benefit substantially.

Recruiting

Recruiting is, of course, only necessary if the peer assessment project is voluntary. The project organizer must decide whether all the class are to be involved, or whether to start with a small group of volunteers and use them as a model of enjoyment that will persuade the rest of the class of the desirability of joining in a little later. There is some advantage in leaving the more diffident children to consider their decision at leisure, since a definite positive commitment will certainly get the project off to a better start. Public demonstration is the most potent form of advertising.

In a project involving same-age peer assessment within a single class, recruitment will be no problem. At least half of the class will readily volunteer when the nature of the exercise is briefly described. As noted above, your difficulty will be that these are unlikely to be a representative group. You will have to think about how you might stratify this to obtain a representative group.

Where helped or helpers do not already exist as a naturalistic group, they may need to be approached individually. In this circumstance, a clear form of words should be prepared that is used consistently in all invitations, to dispel any anxieties that may be aroused by the initial approach. Contact should preferably be made personally, but some project coordinators have utilized written invitations, and publicity through advertisements on posters and handbills, and in newspapers and magazines. The impact of transmission of good news by word of mouth through the 'grapevine' should not be underestimated.

Parental Agreement

The question of parental agreement often arises in connection with peer assessment projects. Involvement in such a project is usually sufficiently interesting to result in some of the students mentioning it at home. This can result in a few parents getting strange ideas about how teachers are using their time (and their students').

It is thus usually desirable for a brief note from school to be taken home by both helpers and helped, explaining the project very simply and reassuring parents that the project will have both academic and social benefits for helpers as well as helped. If a regular home–school newsletter exists, mention of the project there might be sufficient. The necessary minimum of information should be given, couched in a simple and straightforward but reassuring format. (See "Information for Parents," Table 3.1, which is intended to serve this purpose. To enable you to print out this table, you can find it at www.routledge.com/9780815367659. It may be copied, or you may just choose to use bits of it.)

Incentives/Reinforcement

Particularly in North America, some peer assessment projects have incorporated some form of payment or tangible reward for helpers, and sometimes tangible rewards for the helped. This is, however, very unusual in Europe, and there are clearly cultural differences in expectations, quite apart from the question of availability of finance to support this.

The majority of organizers of peer assessment projects prefer to rely on the intrinsic motivation of helpers and helped alike, using tangible extrinsic reinforcement sparingly, only with students who really need such measures, and then only to engineer an initial "flying start." Extrinsic tangible reinforcement should rarely be necessary. Some project organizers do utilize badges of identification, certificates of merit and effort, and very small "prizes" such as pens, but these have much more import at the social psychological level as a token of esteem and an indicator of belonging than as any form of tangible reward.

Social Reinforcement and Modeling

Peer assessment does, of course, include a great deal of "social reinforcement" by way of praise, both private and public. Students will differ in their preferences for public vs. private praise. In a group setting, it is also likely to involve "vicarious reinforcement" – students observing that peer assessment

Table 3.1 Information for Parents

PEER ASSESSMENT: A BRIEF GUIDE

Part of life at school asks children to try to do better than other children. But another very important part of school and later life is working with and helping other people. Children learn well in both ways.

What is Peer Assessment?

Peer assessment means having children try to help other children to learn by appraising or assessing their work – then encouraging each other to think about and discuss what makes a good piece of work. After this discussion the piece of work is likely to be revised before it is submitted for final assessment.

Both the child who is assessed and the child who is the assessor are likely to be helped by this process. It is important that peer assessment is set up in a way that makes sure that this happens. So helpers are not just being "used." To be able to help you have to really get to understand the subject well and be able to explain it. So helping helps the helpers learn faster, too.

Sometimes older children help younger children, and sometimes more able children help less able children of the same age. Usually however, peer assessment operates between children of the same age and ability, and it is reciprocal – that is, each partner takes turns to assess the other partner.

Peer assessment is used for only a small part of the school day. It increases the effectiveness of regular teaching directly by the class teacher, which still forms by far the biggest part of schooling.

The idea is a very old one, first noted hundreds of years ago. Teachers in many different kinds of schools have found that peer assessment is a great "boost" for all children. Today, peer assessment is spreading rapidly in many parts of the world.

Does It Work?

Peer assessment has been used with a very wide range of subjects, including mathematics, spelling, writing, languages,

(continued)

(continued)

science, thinking skills, and computer skills. There is a lot of research over many years proving that peer assessment works. The helpers improve in the subject area as much, if not more than, the students who are helped, but at their own level. Research shows that peer assessment also improves how both helper and helped feel about the subject area – they get to like it more. Also, in many cases the helper and helped grow to like each other more, and get on better. There are also many reports of both helper and helped showing more confidence. The research clearly shows that peer assessment is a highly effective way of using school time.

Planning

Peer assessment takes time and care to set up properly, and it is the professional teacher who has the skill to do this. Careful plans must be made for matching students, finding the right sort of materials, training helping and helped students, and many other points of organization. Like any other way of effective teaching, setting up peer helper projects needs enthusiasm, careful planning and hard work on the part of the teacher. Peer assisted learning is not an easy option.

is visibly socially rewarding for other students, and therefore believing that such rewards can also be gained by themselves.

Teachers should seek to publicly highlight the important components of praiseworthy behavior quite specifically, to capitalize on this effect. The progressive introduction of component skills required to perform well, and immediate repeated practice at using these newly acquired skills, will also be important for less able students. Younger and less able children have difficulty attending to modeled events for long periods, distinguishing relevant from irrelevant cues, and organizing information. They are also more easily swayed by the immediate consequences of their actions, whereas older and more able students can generally keep longer-term goals in mind and are more likely to perform actions consistent with their goals and values.

Seeing others succeed or fail, or be rewarded or punished, creates outcome expectations, and students are more likely to perform actions when they believe they will be successful or rewarded than when they expect to fail or be punished. However, students' interpretations of reinforcement of others may depend on their confidence and belief in their ability to reproduce the reinforced behaviors.

Students often learn new skills and strategies by observing models. Peer models are most influential in situations where perceived similarity to the model provides information about one's own abilities and the appropriateness of behaviors. Observing competent models perform actions that lead to success conveys information about the sequence of actions to use to succeed. By observing modeled behaviors and their consequences, people form outcome expectations about which behaviors are likely to be rewarded or punished, and people's actions are based on their expectations. Of course, some students will lack the ability to identify the important features of modeled acts or the meaning of modeled responses, and this will need scaffolding by the teacher.

The most effective models are thus probably those who are not generally more competent than their observers, but who become competent at performing modeled responses over time. Such peer models are 'proximal' and credible in that they have started where the observer currently is, and model not only current competence, but also step-wise strategies to achieve that level of competence, and (importantly) the socio-emotional aspects of "coping." This might be particularly important with students who have a history of learning failure.

E. Helping Technique

Naturally, the helping technique you choose to use will need to be appropriate for the chronological and developmental age of the target students, both helpers and helped. At an early stage, you also need to decide whether to opt for fixed or reciprocal peer assessment, since that engages with decisions about same-ability or cross-ability matching, as well as with decisions about the type of helping technique to be used.

Think about whether the task to be peer assessed is relatively surface or complex. Start peer assessment with a relatively simple task. Then develop it into something more complex later. Make sure the assessment criteria are clear and preferably written into some sort of memo, schedule or a rubric. Do involve the students in developing the criteria, even if they end up with something very like what you would have given them anyway. Do not have too many assessment criteria.

Do you intend to scaffold interaction between the peer assessment partners with guiding prompts, sentence openers, cue cards or other scaffolding – if so have these prepared well in advance as you will need to give them out during training. You might have different levels of complexity for partners with different levels of ability. What will be the role of questioning in the discussion between the partners, and do you need to scaffold that questioning, at least at the beginning? Make clear that it is not just the assessor who asks questions, but the assessee is also welcome to ask questions of the assessor. What you are aiming for is a roughly equal amount of talk between assessor and assessee – if the assessor is doing all the talking you will need to intervene and coach the assessee in talking more.

Will the peer assessment to be face-to-face or online? If online, will it be synchronous or asynchronous? Do you want to set some parameters for quality of feedback, positive initially then perhaps positive and negative later? Perhaps three positive statements, then three mentions of areas where some improvement might make the piece better.

What about the nature of feedback? Is it to be oral in discussion, or is it to be written? Or perhaps the assessors should have a moment to reflect and write down their statements, to aid their fluency when they get into discussion. Are the assessors asked to not only give elaborated verbal feedback but with some sort of quantitative score or grade? In this case they will certainly need some reflection time before writing down their comments and their grades. Will the elaborated feedback be specific and concise or vague and general – or both? Will it be reinforcing, suggestive, didactic or corrective? Will justification of feedback be expected? This might be difficult at first but should be prompted for later.

Are the participants clear about the degree of reworking expected? In other words, are revisions to be few or many, simple or complex? The constraint here will be time available, so you might want to put a quota on time and also suggest a limit on number of changes. Once students are more familiar with peer assessment, they can move from a highly structured activity to one which is more open to student interpretation.

Peer assessment might be convergent (as in the assessment of whether a student has the correct answer to a mathematics problem), or divergent (as in the assessment of the quality and value of a piece of creative writing). The latter is, of course, much more demanding of the assessor. Especially initially, participants need a clear explanation and demonstration of just what it is they have to do. What, with whom, where, when, with what materials and why are the key questions needing an answer – not necessarily in that order.

The availability of clear assessment criteria does not guarantee their successful application, which requires transfer from knowledge to skill. Providing effective peer assessment requires a complex battery of cognitive, meta-cognitive, and social skills – and in some cases a developmental sequence of learning over weeks coupled with intensive coaching from the teacher.

Peer assessment feedback should be descriptive, balanced, specific, and non-judgmental. In all circumstances, the assessor must understand the goals of the task, recognize progress towards the goal, judge the potential efficacy of addressing gaps in knowledge or strategy in attaining that goal, and be sensitive to the person to whom feedback is given.

General Helping Skills

Some workers have tried to avoid the rigidity sometimes inherent in very highly structured techniques by training helpers in more general helping skills. These could include how to present tasks, how to give clear explanations, how to demonstrate tasks and skills, how to prompt or lead assessees into imitating skills, how to check on helped performance, how to give feedback on performance, how to identify consistent patterns of error or problem in responses, and how to develop more intensive remedial procedures for those patterns of error, for instance. This range of skills is considerably sophisticated. Nevertheless, particularly where relatively able and mature helpers are being used, programs have taken such wide ranging training on board.

Training in ways of giving clear instructions without unnecessary elaboration or the use of difficult vocabulary has been included. The appropriate point at which to resort to demonstration of the requisite skill is covered, with details of how and when prompts should be used. Helpers have been trained in how to observe responses closely, how to give encouraging but accurate feedback regarding the response, and how to respond differentially to different kinds of response. Other relevant helper skills have included the identification of areas where the helped student needs extra help, systematic mastery checking, record keeping, and the ability to deal with 'take-homes' and home back-up reinforcers.

All of this sounds complicated and ambitious, but care must be taken not to underestimate the abilities of helpers, potential or actual. Many helpers may be well versed in a variety of helping behaviors in other environments, and for many of them training and helping behaviors will merely require the development or shaping of more precise skills from existing repertoires of behavior, rather than instruction from a baseline of no skill at all.

General Social Skills

Because peer assessment involves interaction, social skills inevitably play a part. Teachers might wish to prepare for the introduction of peer assessment by introductory work with the class on friendship and its meanings and implications. Any preliminary activities that serve to foster a collaborative ethos among the students should prove useful. Including social "ice-breakers" as part of first encounters in training meetings might be desirable. This can develop to the greater complexities of establishing rapport, sharing interest, verbal and non-verbal social skills, and so on.

Helping involves a very subtle social process. Some programs take pains to instruct helpers in the establishing of an initial rapport, giving hints on the initiation of conversation, discovering something about the helped and their interests, the importance of revealing things about oneself in order that the helped may do likewise, and so on. It is obviously important for the helper to learn about the interests of the helped in a variety of areas, especially since discovery of a shared interest will do much to cement the bond between the two. In addition to the verbal and non-verbal social skills involved in praising, the importance of aspects of behavior such as physical proximity, eye contact and posture may be incorporated in initial training for helpers.

The attitudes the helper brings to the task are obviously very important. The importance of positive attitudes in encouraging regular attendance can be emphasized, and considerable attention given to means of establishing good rapport with and stimulating positive motivation in the helped. Sometimes information about the problems of the helped is given to the helpers in order to develop empathy. Equally, helpers have sometimes been advised about the dangers of feeling too "sympathetic" towards the helped, and falling too readily into the trap of providing unconscious prompts and excessive help, which might foster over-dependence.

Criteria

For peer assessment the establishment of clear and specific criteria will be necessary, to enable helpers to determine reliably whether a particular student behavior or response or artifact does or does not fall within a particular category. Clearly defined criteria on performance dimensions are likely to be better accepted by students. The nature of the criteria will, of course, vary greatly according to the curricular output to be assessed and the objectives of the exercise. Helpers will always need multiple exemplars of application of these criteria. Written prompts or reminders should also be provided. However, teachers must also be alert to the possibility of some students' using written criteria and checklists very rigidly and procedurally, limiting the quality of discourse and providing feedback that is rather sterile.

Some teachers advocate the use of rubrics to structure interactions in peer assessment. Carefully designed guidelines or question protocols are likely to improve the quality of interaction by prompting elaborated explanations and providing students with an appropriate language to convey their thoughts. In guided questioning procedures, students develop their own questions about specific topics from generic question "stems."

Teachers will vary the level of structure according to the developmental level and experience of the students involved. For example, inexperienced students could initially be provided with a list of relatively convergent criteria to apply in assessing one another's work (e.g. uses tense appropriately), but subsequently be encouraged to use more divergent criteria.

If helpers have participated in the development of the criteria, they are likely to feel a greater sense of ownership and better motivation. Criteria developed jointly with students are also more likely to be expressed in language which the students can understand. The opportunity to access a second opinion from another peer assessor or the teacher, and discuss the key features of any assessed artifact regarding the boundaries of criteria, should always be available.

Correction Procedure

Errors imply failure, and failure creates stress, and stress can produce a negative reaction in the helped, and possibly also in a helper who feels that errors are an indication of incompetence on their part. To avoid irritation, frustration and disharmony in the helping relationship, all peer assessment techniques should include some form of pre-specified error correction procedure. Otherwise you might have peer assessors rushing in and declaring "that is wrong!" in a very unhelpful way.

Whatever this is, it needs to be quick, simple and consistently applicable, easy, and non-stressful for both children. The helper might then go on to prompt their partner to offer alternatives, and comment on those alternatives. Very rarely should the helper give their partner the "right" answer – or what they think is the right answer, since this encourages dependence, and might even lead to further error.

Master Reference Source

If you are operating a convergent form of peer assessment, in which definite "right answers" do exist, you should consider whether the helpers should be able to access those correct answers in some way (e.g., by referring to the correct solutions often given at the back of textbooks of math problems). This is only likely to be possible where the peer assessment participants are working with materials from a prepared finite pool, to which model answers are available. Providing some master reference source of correct responses might be particularly necessary in forms of peer assessment in which the helper's mastery of the curriculum area might be in doubt. It might also prove particularly useful during the practice element of initial training for peer assessment where the practice is done with standardized items for all participants.

For example, in training for peer assessment of writing, when using a standard piece of anonymous writing for practice purposes for all participants, a master reference version could be provided to helpers with all the errors of mechanics highlighted (spelling, punctuation, syntax, etc). However, this should only be done toward the end of the practice session, so helpers could then self-assess their independent level of "accuracy" and competence, and ensure their partner had been given full and proper feedback.

Praise

Specification is needed of the nature, frequency and circumstances for usage of praise in the helping relationship. It is useful to specify some sort of minimum frequency with which praise should be deployed, but even more important to give a clear indication of those circumstances in which it should always be used. Many helpers find that the giving of verbal praise does not come naturally to them, and they may need considerable practice and feedback in this before an adequate level of performance is achieved. In training, the verbal and non-verbal aspects of praise should be emphasized, since the use of routine praise words in a boring monotone will not have the desired effect.

In addition, in some helping relationships the use of a pat on the back or some other gesture may serve to add variety to the social reinforcement. Some helpers have a very restricted vocabulary of praise words, and part of helper training could include a listing of appropriate vocabulary. In addition to verbal and non-verbal praise, the record keeping inherent in the project organization may include an element of written praise from both helpers and supervising professionals.

Trouble Shooting

It may be worthwhile producing some sort of simple directory of common problems with some indication of how these may be solved. Even if this is not made available in written form to the helpers as a training resource, it will serve as a very handy reference for you. You may rest assured that there will be constant additions to this collection with every subsequent project, for no two projects are quite the same. It will be worthwhile making clear at the outset that problems may arise which are not the fault of either helper or helped. The pair should work on the assumption that if the relationship or process is not working satisfactorily, there is something wrong with the design of the materials or the design of the technique, and they should seek teacher advice in order that appropriate adjustments can be made.

F. Contact

Is peer assessment contact to be scheduled, or allowed to occur spontaneously as needed? Scheduling is almost always necessary in the early weeks of a project, in order to assure that partners have sufficient regular and frequent practice time to consolidate their peer assessment skills and that the teacher can be on hand to monitor their performance and give them feedback and extra coaching as needed. Once the teacher is certain that partners are skillful and confident enough to work with much less support and supervision, allowing them to engage in peer assessment at times of their own choosing becomes possible. Naturally, the nature of contact you choose to allow will need to be appropriate for the chronological and developmental age of the target students, both helpers and helped.

The teacher might choose to launch a peer assessment project by training everyone together, then schedule peer assessment time for different sub-groups within the class at different times. This does, however, require the teacher to be doing peer assessment monitoring with one sub-group and other activities simultaneously with other sub-groups. There is always the risk that the quality of peer assessment monitoring will suffer. Consequently, most teachers find it easier to have all their students doing peer assessment simultaneously. However, designating regular routine peer assessment days or sessions might be restrictive. Partners might instead become familiar with the notion that peer assessment always follows certain activities, whenever those activities occur.

Time

A basic decision is whether the peer assessment is to occur wholly in class time, wholly in the children's recess or break time, or in a combination of both. If the helping is to occur entirely in class time, it can be kept under teacher supervision, but will usually require time-tabling, which may rob the exercise of a degree of spontaneity. If the helping is to occur in the children's recess or break time, some very mature pairs can be left to make their own arrangements, but this is a much greater imposition on helpers and helped alike, and the momentum of the project may begin to peter out as the novelty begins to wear off. Some time-tabling may thus be necessary even during the children's recess or leisure time, so that the size and nature of the commitment involved is visible to all from the outset.

The best arrangement may well be to schedule a basic minimum of contact during class time, but make available the possibility for helping pairs to negotiate further sessions in their own break time according to their own levels of enthusiasm. Some projects have arranged for contact after school, or indeed before school starts in the morning. Such arrangements are, of course, highly constrained by the transport arrangements for homeward-bound children and should only be attempted if the enthusiasm of the participants is high.

Place

Most peer assessment takes place in schools, but it can also be found in libraries, community centers, and other neighborhood locations that have easy access. Finding the physical space to accommodate the partners can be a problem. In a cross-age project within one school, particularly where two full classes are involved, it is possible for half of the pairs to work in the classroom of the helped students and the other half in the helpers' classroom. Finding physical space for the helping to occur during recess or break times may be considerably more difficult if there are problems of recess time supervision and/or children are not allowed access to classrooms.

Clearly, a positive social atmosphere is more likely to be fostered if the children have adequate personal space and are comfortable during their helping. An ambience with a degree of informality is therefore preferable, but the situation should not be so informal as to incorporate many distractions from the helping process. A much used leisure area with heavy passing traffic is therefore unlikely to be satisfactory.

Noise too may be a problem. In peer assessment within one classroom, the noise generated by 15 or so pairs of enthusiastic children engaged in lively discussion can be quite considerable.

This is exacerbated in a school with an open internal design, and may generate complaints from other classes who are pursuing a more formal curriculum. It is worth checking the degree of noise transmission, in order to be prepared for this type of complaint.

The availability of an adequate quantity of comfortable seating can also be problematic. Even in a simple project, to find enough chairs that may be situated side by side and are reasonably comfortable for both participants might not be easy. Where the peer assessment is more formal and incorporates some paper and pencil work, the availability of tables also has to be considered. Seating arrangements need to be such that the mobility of professional supervisors will not be impaired. In cross-institution peer assessment, the "imported" students will need to be briefed about the layout of the building, and shown round – this is, of course, ideally done by other students.

Duration

Each individual helping period should last for a minimum of 15 minutes of time actually on task. Little worthwhile can occur in less time than this, after you have allowed for some lack of punctuality and general settling down. If it is possible for those who so desire to continue for 20–30 minutes, this is advantageous. Helping sessions of 30 minutes certainly seem to be the most common period found in the literature. It might be possible for the peer assessment to occur just before a natural recess or break time, with provision for the helping pairs to continue into their own recess time if they so desire.

Helping periods as long as 60 minutes are very unusual, and it would be rare for helping to be scheduled as long as this. It is always better to leave the helping pair less than exhausted and still a little hungry at the end of their joint experience, in order that they will come to their next session with positive attitudes and high energy levels. So, you might start your project with shorter contact times and lengthen these as the participants become more practiced. Some pairs will finish their peer assessment task before the end of the scheduled session, so it is wise to have other activities to hand to keep them productively occupied.

Frequency

To ensure that a project has a significant impact, the frequency of helping contact needs to be at least twice per week, especially in the early weeks when the partners are still developing fluency with the method, and need close monitoring and further coaching. Contact frequency of this order is very commonly found in the literature. However, if more weekly contacts can be arranged **and** student motivation can be sustained at this frequency, so much the better. Children involved in peer helper projects rarely object to daily helping, as most of them find it interesting and rewarding. Some pairs may organize their own impromptu sessions in their own recess or break time whether the teacher mandates this or not. Some projects have incorporated twice daily contacts, but this is rare. Although the literature suggests that the greater the frequency of helping sessions, the more impact a project is likely to have, nevertheless a point of diminishing marginal returns may be found.

Project Period

The peer assessment project should be launched with reference to an initial fixed period of commitment. It is useful for both helpers and helped to be clear about what they are letting themselves in for, and how long a course they need to be able to sustain. Additionally, the literature suggests that short-term projects tend to generate bigger effect sizes. Although this may be merely due to capitalization on sheer novelty, teachers are much less inclined than academics to be dismissive about the value of the Hawthorne Effect (the tendency for the introduction of any new form of organization to produce short-term increments in performance).

So, a minimum project period of six weeks is suggested, since it would barely be possible to discern significant impact in less time than this. Popular project periods are eight weeks and ten weeks, which fit comfortably within an average term or semester, and it is not usually desirable to fix a period of longer than 12 weeks for an initial commitment. It will be much better to review the project at the end of a short initial period, and to obtain feedback from the participants and evaluate the outcomes, and at that stage make conscious joint decisions about improvements or future directions. One thing to definitely avoid is letting the whole thing drift on interminably until it runs out of steam.

G. Materials

Peer assessment has the advantage that it requires very little by way of special materials, other than a list of criteria, and perhaps a list of prompts and a recording form.

Structure

In some forms of peer assessment, highly structured materials are used to guide the interactive behavior of the partners. In other forms of peer assessment, the emphasis is much more upon training in highly structured but generally applicable interactive behaviors, which can then be applied to any relevant materials which are available. There is some evidence that peer assessment is more effective in raising attainment when structured materials are used than in other circumstances. However, considerable costs may be involved in the preparation of such materials. Also, project organizers should beware of the introduction of so much structure that the responses of helper and helped alike become rigid and mechanical.

Difficulty and Choosing

A related question concerns the control of the difficulty level of the materials. Some projects have allowed some choice by the helped and/or helper from a variety of materials that are, nevertheless, compressed to be within bands of difficulty – and the band of difficulty for the partners can be chosen by the teacher or figured out by themselves.

Availability and Sources

In some circumstances it may be possible for the pairs to make some materials, if not for their own use then perhaps for other pairs, but if this is done the project organizer needs to be satisfied that such joint manufacturing is in itself serving an educational purpose. A further consideration is the cost of consumables, and some projects involve the consumption of a substantial stock of paper, worksheets etc.

H. Training

Staff Training

Before teachers set out to train children in particular procedures, it is clearly important that teachers themselves are well versed in the methods to be used. All the relevant professionals need to be fully conversant with the technique in use, including some experience at actually doing it themselves. You will need to have practiced the technique yourself on a child or colleague before trying to disseminate the method further.

Participant Training – Organization

Training the students individually or in pairs may be highly effective, but would be extremely time-consuming and there-fore not efficient, so most teachers opt to train the participants in groups. The strong recommendation is to train helpers and helped together from the outset. By so doing, you ensure that both helpers and helped receive exactly the same message. In tailoring your training so that the helped understand it, you will also improve its accessibility to the less able of the helpers. Importantly, training partners together from the start conveys the immediate impression that "we are all in this together". Training meetings must always lead on immediately to direct practice of the techniques to be utilized, which is another rea-son for having helpers and helped together from the start.

Venue and Space

You will need to specify the date, time and place of your train-ing sessions, with number of training sessions, their length and frequency. This allows the helpers and helped to look forward to their experience and (perhaps) become excited about the impending novel event. It also allows you to make very sure that colleagues are not going to claim the space you intend to use for practice for a last minute play rehearsal or some such.

The physical space in which training is going to occur will need the facility for all the participants to sit in a large group and listen to a talk and watch a demonstration, but there will also be a need for chairs (and possibly tables) to be available for subsequent practice, if this is to be incorporated in the same session (rather than taking place back in their regular classrooms). Thus, plenty of seats need to be available and their mobility to fulfill two purposes should be considered. Remember that noise levels can be a problem, especially in the early stages of training when helpers and helped will not have learnt to modulate their volume.

Materials and Equipment

If audio-visual equipment (e.g. video) is to be used during the training session, the requisite equipment must be: not in use elsewhere, transportable to the location of the training, in good working order and compatible with basic utilities in the training space. The materials to be used for the training session will also need to be readily and reliably available. For the actual practice it will be much better if the specific items and tasks for use by each pair during the practice session have been pre-selected, thus avoiding much student meandering while hunting for an appropriate item. Even in projects where the helpers or helped are in general to be given a fairly free choice of materials and tasks, paradoxically the training meeting may be the one occasion where you need to control the difficulty level of the materials more rigidly.

Participant Training – Content

Training might last as little as 30 minutes in total, although somewhat longer is usual. This might be in one block, or spread over a number of shorter step-wise sessions. If the helpers and helped have not met previously, you will want to allow time for general introductions, and perhaps some co-operative ice-breaker activity in the working partnerships. Some teachers like to inject humor to relax the atmosphere, perhaps through a "how not to do it" role play by a pair of adults or students from a previous project.

Verbal Instruction

Some teachers tend to over-estimate the impact talking to children (lecturing) has upon subsequent behavior. Equally, teachers often over-estimate the ease with which children can assimilate information reliably from written materials. In fact, direct verbal instruction and written instruction (in pamphlets or lists of 'dos and don'ts') cannot be assumed to be effective training methods on their own, although they do form essential components of any training procedure.

Certainly a verbal explanation of the overall structure and purposes of the project will be given by way of introduction, followed by further detailed explanation of the techniques to be used. But keep it brief! Many children, particularly those with any learning difficulty, will be 'switching off' after ten minutes of listening, if not earlier. Take care that the vocabulary you use in your verbal instruction is simple, and that any more unusual words you use are carefully defined for the children (e.g., assessor and assessee). Some project coordinators prefer to substitute words like 'helper' and 'helped'.

Written Instruction

Written instruction may take the form of continuous prose in a pamphlet, but problems of assimilation may arise for some children. Obviously, the reading level of the pamphlet should be kept as low as possible, since it is desirable that both helper and helped are able to refer to it subsequently to check anything of which they may be unsure. However, it may be much more useful to use various forms of checklist, a list of key words or cues, flow charts, diagrams, pictures or cartoons, and so on. For essential reminders about the most important "rules," class wall posters or individual "cue cards" may be helpful. Peer assessors will need assessment criteria, possibly definitions of those criteria, and probably some sort of assessment schedule or rubric. It is worth remembering the old adage that nobody reads anything that cannot be contained on one side of a piece of paper. People often do not turn over the page.

Demonstration

It may be worthwhile allowing some time for questions and discussion. However, many of the issues arising could probably more readily be dealt with by proceeding rapidly to a demonstration of the required behavior. This could be from a videotape available externally, or (more convincingly) one made in school. However, it is often possible for teachers to demonstrate how to use the technique. This could be done with another teacher playing the role of the student to be helped. It is much safer to do this with another teacher or volunteer adult, since if they do not give a perfect demonstration (which is highly likely), you will be able to criticize them in front of the children in a way that would be problematic with a student actor. Additionally, an adult actor is likely to be more visible and audible to a large group in a training meeting.

To demonstrate peer assessment of writing, a sample piece of work can be shown on an overhead (retro) projector, and assessment of its strengths and weaknesses demonstrated by a teacher, who "thinks aloud" through the process and highlights the relevant sections as the assessment proceeds.

Guided Practice and Feedback

Immediate practice of the helping technique is essential, and feedback and coaching should be given by the professionals as soon as possible. In some projects, helpers practice the helping technique by role play on each other before being exposed to the helped, and this may be a useful form of organization if the helping technique is particularly complex. In most cases however, it should be possible to proceed directly to practice in the intended helper/helped pairs.

In peer assessment practice sessions, a standard piece of work might be used for all pairs to practice on together (or one of three pieces of work of various complexity, depending on their relative ability), and the partners asked to think aloud, discuss and highlight this anonymous item, before attempting to apply the same principles to a real piece of their own real work. Or you might feel they could cope immediately with applying peer assessment to a real piece of their own work within the practice session.

Checking and Coaching

The behavior of the partners needs close monitoring during the practice session, and this can put a considerable strain on staffing resources. In a practice session of 20 minutes, a professional cannot expect to observe in detail the helping technique of more than five or six pairs. Thus, if large groups are being trained, a substantial number of 'checkers' who are conversant with the techniques will need to be available – this is undoubtedly the most labor-intensive part of the training procedure.

Those partners who demonstrate that they have learned the procedures rapidly can be praised and left to continue, but those partners who are struggling or using deviant technique will need immediate extra individual coaching until they have fully mastered the procedures. Typically, each checker is likely to find that two of the six pairs they are monitoring have learnt the technique extremely well and merely require social reinforcement, another two will have the technique more or less right albeit rather shakily but are thought to be likely to improve with a little practice, while a further two will be doing something aberrant, and may need to be helped individually through considerable unlearning before a virtual re-teaching of the technique from scratch can occur. Much time will be spent with these last two pairs.

Organization and Contracting

Once the children have gained mastery of the technique, they will need briefing about the organizational "nuts and bolts" of the day-to-day running of the project. This will include details about access to materials, means of record keeping, arranging times and places for helping contact, and the procedures for further help and follow up. A brief written reminder of these organizational details may be helpful.

I. Process Monitoring

Especially in a first project, close monitoring will be essential to ensure that the maximum benefit is gained by all participants. During the course of the project, it is important that the coordinating teacher keeps a close eye on how things are going, in order to be able to:

- nip any incipient problems in the bud
- dispense plentiful praise and enthusiasm to keep motivation high
- ensure that technique does not show signs of "drift"
- check that the peer assessment partners are maintaining positive social relationships
- be sure that materials used are from an appropriate sequence/level of difficulty
- generally review the complexity and richness of the learning taking place.

While careful observation is necessary, no teacher will be able to visit with all the peer assessment partners during one class session. This may take two or even three sessions. However, during this time the partners will be settling down, and they might well solve some of their problems by themselves. The teacher does not have to do everything.

Self-referral

In the spirit of co-operation that permeates peer assessment, the children themselves may be the first to report difficulty or seek help from the teacher. Children should be encouraged to report difficulties readily in accommodating to each other's habits without feeling that they are "telling tales." Participants might be encouraged to refer to other pairs for consultations about minor matters, or the teacher might consider this potentially too disruptive of other pairs. It is also helpful to give the participants a clear notion of the nature and size of problems that they should self-refer, together with some examples. If a participant who is known to be of high status in the peer group can be prompted to be the first to refer a fairly minor problem, the other children will soon follow suit. In some projects, a record is kept of problems arising in order that they may be discussed with all the project participants as a group at a later time.

Self-recording

Some form of recording of tasks completed during the project is highly desirable. Self-recording gives a tangible demonstration of achievement and progress for the children, and is of considerable interest and utility for the supervising teacher. It is entirely logical that these records should be kept by the children themselves. With more wide-ranging helping, simple diaries can be kept by each pair, while projects utilizing much more specific techniques might generate much more precise records. If the record keeping can be shared by helper and helped, then so much the better. Even quite young children prove to be surprisingly good at writing positive comments about their partner, and learning to both give and receive praise without embarrassment is a valuable component of peer assessment projects. By and large, helper comments should be as positive as possible, with any problems discussed directly with the project coordinator via self-referral.

In some cases the helpers soon begin to run out of imagination with respect to their positive comments, and this is an experience that has been shared by teachers who have had to write scores of end-of-year reports. The vocabulary of praise used by helpers can extend much further into the vernacular than a teacher would countenance for themselves, and ideas for praise words can be supplied by the helped student or the comments negotiated between helper and helped, although written down by the helper. Dictionaries of praise words and phrases can be brainstormed and printed, or put on the classroom wall.

The records themselves should be checked each week by the supervising teacher, who can also record some favorable comment and add an official signature, perhaps together with other signs of approval such as points or merit marks for particularly deserving work.

Discussion

Many projects feature review meetings between coordinating teachers and the helpers and helped. These can occur with the helpers and helped separately or together, and with them in groups or as individuals. The general aim is to discuss how the project is going in general, and any further specific problems. Group sessions can be valuable for helpers and/or helped to discover that other pairs are having the same problems as they are. Sometimes regular "de-briefing" meetings have been held between helpers and coordinators.

Direct Observation and Coaching

Close monitoring and some retraining are likely to be necessary for some partners to maintain procedural integrity. Of all the monitoring procedures, direct observation is by far the most revealing. The peer assessment session is not an opportunity for the teacher to "get on with some marking." On the contrary, the teacher should be circulating round the group observing and guiding children as necessary. In addition, it is possible to ask a particularly expert child helper who is not otherwise engaged to act as an observer in a similar way and report back to the teacher.

A simple checklist of the elements of the technique or other procedure may be useful to help to structure these observations. This could be very similar to, although perhaps a little more elaborate than, the written checklist of "rules" or "cues" that could have been given to the peer assessment pairs as part of the initial training procedure. It is also possible to use video or audio recording for monitoring purposes, and this can be very useful for feedback to individual pairs or the group as a whole, as well as being valuable as a training aid for subsequent projects. However it does take time and expertise to arrange and analyze.

Once the partners have settled, it will become easier to see which partners are in need of further coaching, and the teacher can make more specifically purposed visits. Observation is likely to lead to coaching (although not too soon). This can follow the sequence:

- observe and give verbal coaching
- observe + jointly intervene with peer assessor
- intervene individually to show assessor what is required
- return later to check performance.

Each step is only enacted when the previous one has failed to produce a result.

Teachers might wish to assign two assessors to one student to be assessed in cases where there is doubt about the reliability of one assessor, then compare the two independent ratings (taking care to ensure there is no conferring or copying). The teacher might also undertake some direct monitoring themselves, and compare their own data with those of one or two peer assessors.

Some teachers choose to conduct their own assessment of a small sample of work that is peer assessed, rotating through the students week by week until all the pairs have been checked in this way. Some teachers assess the peer assessments and give feedback on them to the assessors, while drawing out general points to communicate to all helpers and helped. Where consistency, reliability and validity of helper judgements are found to be shaky, further discussion and coaching with respect to these issues is clearly needed. Teachers should expect to fade the strength and frequency of their monitoring with most students as the project progresses. However, all students will continue to need some monitoring and prompting, although this can usually become more intermittent.

Project Process

Some form of check on the basic organizational parameters of the project will also be necessary. The attendance of helpers and helped at scheduled contact times might require monitoring. You may find, for instance, that helping sessions scheduled for the very beginning of the school day are affected by irregularities in transport, while those that are scheduled for the end of the school day or after school may be rendered problematic at certain times of the year by inclement weather or dark nights. If review meetings are to be held between peer assessment participants and project coordinators, attendance at these and response in them needs to be noted. Organizational problems must be nipped in the bud at the earliest possible moment, and adjustments or modifications introduced as soon as possible.

Recognition of Successful Students

Teachers often choose to celebrate or publicly recognize students during a peer assessment project. The students that have been recognized will become peer models, so the choice of students to be recognized must be informed by this expectation. There are consequently dangers in publicly acknowledging during the course of the peer assessment activity students who might well have improved in some way but whose performance is still considerably less than perfect. The precise reason or noteworthy aspect of the student's performance that led to the acknowledgement should be specified.

J. Assessment of Students

Teachers will feel a need to examine the quality of peer feedback over time, as well as checking its reliability and validity. It may, of course, start low, become higher, then drop off again as students begin to lose interest and seek some other novelty. Obviously, this information will need to be fed back to the students – feedback information is one of the keys to changing behavior.

Teachers will also feel a need to check learning outcomes, perhaps by direct observation. After all, the main point of peer assessment is not just that it develops appraisal skills, reflection and discussion, but that it enhances attainment in the area of application. Additionally, what social, communicative and other transferable skills can be observed or measured?

Some assessment of student progress in terms of learning outcomes is an automatic by-product of teacher process monitoring, especially by direct observation. The teacher will also be checking on student self-recorded evidence of progress through materials, although this might be less reliable as an indicator that learning has definitely taken place. Additionally, the teacher might make informal observations regarding any changes in general learning behavior or learning style, or note any evidence of improved meta-cognitive awareness in either helpers or helped students (perhaps by eavesdropping on discussions between pairs).

Peer assessment does, of course, serve an assessment function as well as an intervention function. From an assessment perspective, recorded peer assessment data might have diagnostic value for the teacher. Given this assessment function, it is important that the peer assessment data is accurate and reliable. Some peer assessment procedures incorporate peer-administered tests or probes which are integral to helping procedure.

Over the last decade, computer programs of increasing sophistication have become available to assist the teacher with the management of information about learning in the classroom. These forms of computerized curriculum based measurement are both delivered to the student and scored by the computer, which then analyzes the results and advises the teacher of the outcome (and sometimes the diagnostic implications for action). Another development is the availability of norm-referenced tests of attainment, which are delivered, scored and interpreted by the computer. Where such tests have a very large item bank, every test presented to every student on every occasion is different, which not only minimizes student cheating but also enables the tests to be taken very frequently without scores being inflated by practice effects as students get to learn the test content. Such tests are, of course, not as closely tied to the peer assessment curriculum as curriculum-based tests, but can still form a useful measure of student progress in terms of generalization of skills to novel content.

K. Evaluation

Chapter 5 is about Evaluation, and here we simply refer the reader to that chapter. However, evaluation issues will be found in the Organization Template (Table 3.2).

L. Feedback

The monitoring and evaluation information will need collating and summarizing in some way, or (to be more precise) in two ways. A simple way of presenting the favorable results and information to the participants themselves is necessary to encourage them and promote further growth of confidence. A more 'scientific' collation will be necessary to present to interested colleagues. Decisions must be taken about how to summarize the data for the various purposes, what balance of verbal, numerical and graphic presentation to use, and whether to incorporate any analysis of statistical significance or index of effect size (and if so which).

Feedback to the children can be group or individual, with the helpers and helped separate or together. Do not assume that the children will be easily fobbed off by some vague generalizations. They are likely to want something more tangible and structured than that. You must make a decision about whether individual pairs are given information about their own progress (bearing in mind that even if they are not given comparative information they will soon be asking their friends for this), or whether the group as a whole should merely be given information about overall improvement based on group averages.

When evaluation information is given to the participants, it is always useful to make the feedback process reciprocal, and encourage them to give you their views (verbally or in writing or both) on how the project went, and how it could be improved for another generation on a subsequent occasion. Very often, the students will make suggestions that are contradictory, and therefore rather difficult to implement, but some of their suggestions will undoubtedly be insightful and extremely helpful when organizing further projects.

At the end of the initial phase of the project, joint decisions have to be made about the future. At this point, the views of the participants must be taken very much into account. Some may wish to continue peer assessment with the same frequency, some may wish to apply it to another product, others may wish to continue but with lesser frequency, while a few may want a complete rest at least for a while. When in doubt, a good rule of thumb is to go for the parsimonious option. It will be better to leave some of the children a little "hungry" and have them pestering you to launch another project in six weeks' time, rather than let peer assessment meander on indefinitely until it quietly expires in a swamp of indifference.

You may feel it desirable for those helpers and helped who have completed the initial phase of commitment of your project satisfactorily to receive some form of public commendation for their efforts. Teachers might choose to celebrate those who have made most progress from their own individual baseline, or those who exerted the most effort. Acknowledged gains can, of course, be in attainment or in the affective or social domain.

Quite apart from its value as reinforcement for the peer assessment pairs, some form of public commendation is also useful publicity that may assist in the later recruitment of new helpers.

Reassurance

The danger with any form of instruction is, of course, that by breaking a naturally acquired skill into its constituent parts, it promotes the "technicalization" of something that is actually not that difficult. Right now you may well be feeling that organizing peer assessment is a great deal more difficult and complicated than you had first thought, and you might feel that you have gone off the idea.

Be reassured. Many of the potential problems mentioned above will never come to afflict you. Setting up your first peer assessment project will undoubtedly be a great deal easier than you imagined. What we have tried to do here is cover all of the possible points of decision.

At many of these points, you can decide if the item is irrelevant or decide "No," and proceed carefully to organize a very simple project, which will probably be very successful. In this case, your completion of the Organization Template (Table 3.2) will be very brief, and it will have many blank spaces and be sprinkled with "No" or "Not Applicable."

However, if your project should happen to be less successful than you would have liked, you will be able to review your decisions about organization very easily, and determine where you might have gone wrong or left something out that might have been crucial. Thus, if you don't succeed first time, you will certainly succeed at the second attempt. Now at least you are prepared for anything. Well, almost anything.

The next chapter goes from the nuts and bolts of organizing your own project to considering the theory behind peer assessment and the empirical evidence for its effectiveness.

Table 3.2 Peer Assessment Organization Template

This template should help to inform your initial thinking about your peer assessment project, help to structure the agenda of any subsequent collaborative planning meetings, form a useful record of the planning decisions agreed, and enable the consensus decisions to be communicated in a standard form to all the stakeholders.

The template lists the major questions to ask and areas of decision to consider when planning a peer assessment project. You will see that they are laid out under 12 main headings:

A. Context
B. Objectives
C. Curriculum Area
D. Participants
E. Helping Technique
F. Contact
G. Materials
H. Training
I. Process Monitoring
J. Assessment of Students
K. Evaluation
L. Feedback

Do not be alarmed by the apparent size of the template. It lists many options, only some of which will be relevant to you. The template strives for a degree of generality that makes it applicable to all sorts of peer assessment projects, hopefully without losing too much specificity and practicality.

You will find it useful to print off a copy of the template. As and when you make your final decisions, write them on the template as a record. This will constitute a useful organizational summary to copy and distribute to other interested parties. Inevitably, you will find you need more space under some headings than is actually provided. When photocopying the template for onward use, you could enlarge the first version to give yourself more space.

Some of the sections of the template are inter-dependent (e.g. D Selection of Participants and E Technique of Helping). Thus you might not be able to finalize all your decisions in one

(continued)

(continued)

linear pass through the template – you might need to loop back to revisit some sections.

Good luck!

A: The Context

1. Are you in:

   ○ an elementary school?
   ○ a middle school?
   ○ a high school?
   ○ a kindergarten?
   ○ a special school?
   ○ other? (please specify)

2. Problems specific to the situation

   ○ to be addressed by the peer assessment project?
   ○ likely to impair the success of the project?

      i. low motivation and expectation in students, poor goal-setting?
      ii. low standards of attainment?
      iii. poor on-task behavior, students often seeking teacher attention?
      iv. poor inter-group relationships?
      v. high incidence of behavior problems?
      vi. ethnic minorities, second language, special needs?
      vii. inappropriate accommodation, curriculum, teaching methods?
      viii. other?

3. What supports are available:

      i. from teacher colleagues in school?
      ii. from head teacher or other senior teacher(s)?
      iii. from outside agencies and helpers?

   ○ Who will stand in your way? How will you get round this?
   ○ Who will give only verbal support but no action?
   ○ Who will give practical help in time?
   ○ Who will give practical help in resources?

B: Objectives

Specify the objectives of the PAL project:

- formative or summative assessment? Or both?
- or formative leading to summative?
- objectives in observable, operational, and preferably measurable terms
- in what curriculum area (expanded later)?
- with which students (expanded later)?
- in which of the relevant domains:

    ○ attainment (cognitive)
    ○ meta-cognitive (insight into learning processes)
    ○ attitudinal, motivational (affective)
    ○ social
    ○ teacher time saving?

For the helpers:

i.

ii.

iii.

For the helped:

i.

ii.

iii.

    ○ How does this align with existing instructional goals and objectives?
    ○ Do you think it is feasible, or is it over-ambitious? Keep it simple to start!
    ○ Do you think you and your students will enjoy doing it?

C: Curriculum Area and Products to Be Peer Assessed

- reading – oral reading? word recognition? decoding? comprehension?
- language – expressive and/or receptive?
- thinking skills and problem solving
- writing – creative or technical? single item or portfolio?
- spelling – words or general skills?

(continued)

(continued)

- second, other and foreign languages
- mathematics
- science
- information and communication technology skills
- physical education
- music
- other (the possibilities are endless):

What products will be assessed? For example:

- writing
- drawing
- oral statements
- presentations
- portfolios
- movement
- performance
- other?

  - Please be specific when you define the products.
  - Will there be single or multiple assessments?
  - How will this align with and complement the mainstream curriculum? (Your head teacher will ask this question!)
  - How might this conflict with the mainstream curriculum?
  - What will peer assessment during class time displace (in other words, what will you not do to enable you to do peer assessment)?

D: Selection and Matching of Participants

1. Arrangements to introduce peer assessment to students gently

   - How will you deal with student resistance?
   - Will there be cultural resistances?
   - Do students understand/expect interdependence?
   - Is there a supportive classroom climate?
   - Is there a degree of trust and psychological safety?
   - Voluntary or compulsory? Or voluntary initially?

2. Structural Factors:

   - within or between institutions or buildings?
   - within or between classes?
   - class-wide or a selected sub-group?

3. Background Factors:
   - Experience of students? Pre-existing skills?
   - Previous experience positive or negative?
   - Current maturity, work habits, co-operative ethos, etc.

   Helpers: Helped:
4. Matching selective, random or accidental?
5. Age:

   same-age or cross-age (cross-grade) helpers?
6. Numbers of Participants (target totals)

   Helpers: Helped:
7. Contact Constellation

   Assessors individuals, pairs or groups (what size?)?

   Assessees individuals, pairs or groups (what size?)?

   _____ helpers to   _____ helped
8. Ability
   - cross-ability or same-ability? (same-ability to start?)
   - ? range of ability in: Helpers: Helped:
   - how do you know this? what indicators for ranking?
   - how to maintain a helper/helped differential?
   - special needs?   Helpers: Helped:
   - special strengths?   Helpers: Helped:
9. Fixed or reciprocal roles?
10. Social Factors
   - how to accommodate existing positive or negative relationships?
   - how to accommodate weak and strong personalities?
11. Gender

   same-sex or cross-sex matching?
12. Participant Partner Preference

   accept to what degree if at all?   Helpers: Helped:
13. Standby Helpers

   back-up/spare/supply helpers to cover absence/dropout?

   From?   How many?

   (continued)

(continued)

14. Recruiting (if voluntary)

    in person, in writing, advertising, publicity, grapevine?

    Helpers: Helped:

15. Parental Agreement

    necessary? How much information to give?

    Helpers: Helped:

16. Incentives/Reinforcement

    for recruiting, necessary?

    For helpers?   For helped?

17. Peer assessment to be confidential or public?
18. Peer assessment partner(s) to be anonymous or known?

E: Helping Technique

- Task surface or complex, or developing from one to another?
- Assessment criteria clear?
- Students involved in developing and clarifying assessment criteria?
- Will there be an assessment rubric?
- Peer assessment to be face-to-face or online, synchronous or asynchronous?
- Interaction with guiding prompts, sentence openers, cue cards or other scaffolding devices?
- Role of questioning in feedback? By assessor, assessee?
- Equal talk and discussion – assessor not "expert"?
- Quantity of feedback?
- Nature of feedback (oral, written, etc.)?
- Elaborated and specific or concise and general?
- Feedback positive, negative, or both?
- Feedback quantitative or qualitative or both?
- Feedback reinforcing, suggestive, didactic or corrective?
- Justification of feedback expected? (Think before you speak!)
- Participants clear about degree of reworking?
- Revisions to be few or many, simple or complex?
- Activity highly structured (initially) or student interpreted (later)?

- General helping skills relevant?
  - e.g. presentation, explanation, modeling, demonstration, prompting, checking, error identification, process monitoring, assessment, feedback, remediation
- General social skills relevant?
  - e.g. establishing rapport, sharing interest, verbal and non-verbal social skills, etc.
- Praise
  - specify frequency of, and circumstances for, praise.
  - verbal and non-verbal, must be genuine! - and how to avoid criticizing.
- Trouble-shooting
  - what do they do if they hit problems?

F: Contact

1. Scheduled or as-needed?

   if latter, how ensure initial fluency in technique?
2. Whole class simultaneously or rotating groups?
3. Time
   - class time/recess or break time/both/after school?
   - times fixed for all or various by negotiation?
4. Place
   - school or other center?
   - classroom/leisure or play area/other?
   - outside school? Homes, community centers, libraries?
   - consider movement or transport implications
   - check seating availability and acoustic absorbency (noise!)
5. Duration

   15, 20, 30, 45, 60 minutes?
6. Frequency

   3, 4, 5, 10 times weekly?
7. Project Period

   6, 8, 10 weeks, 1 semester (term), longer?

(continued)

(continued)

8. Problems

   o in cross-age/class/institution helping, how to match timetables?
   o and how much disruption from student movement?

9. Other Activities

   o for students who do not wish to participate?
   o for PAL students who finish early?

G: Materials

Materials may be simple and readily available. Or they may not be readily available and need to be obtained.

1. Origin

   o regular classroom materials?
   o specially made materials?
   o students or adults to prepare specially made materials?

2. Structure

   highly structured and sequenced or flexible and open-ended?

3. Difficulty

   finely graded and of controlled difficulty?

4. Choosing

   o open choice, or open within a specific level?
   o how much choosing practice before giving guidance?

5. Availability

   o expensive hardware required? Cost of consumables?
   o can pairs or other volunteers make materials?

6. Sources

   o in-house existing materials
   o library loan
   o special collection
   o import from other establishments
   o material from participants' homes?

7. Access
   - how frequent and easy is access to the materials?
   - who takes the initiative on access, helper or helped or other?

8. Progression
   - who determines when to move onto other material, and how?

9. Recording
   - what recording system for loan/possession of materials?
   - is it quick and efficient?
   - handled by specialist or by helpers/helped?
   - who replenishes stock gone missing?

H: Training

1. Staff Training

   all relevant professionals fully conversant with materials and techniques?

2. Participant Training – Organization

   i. Grouping
      - individual or group?
      - assessors and assessees separately or together or both?

   ii. Venue
      - date/time/place?
      - number/length of sessions?

   iii. Audio-visual Equipment
      - available/working?
      - other teaching aids?

   iv. Materials
      - available, pre-selected?
      - controlled for practice?

   v. Practice Space

      check seats/noise levels

(continued)

(continued)

3. Participant Training – Content

    i. Verbal Instruction

       keep it brief!

    ii. Written Instruction

        pamphlets, checklists, flowcharts, reminders

    iii. Demonstration

        from teacher (role play) or experienced helper or on video

    iv. Guided Practice and Feedback

        helpers and helped directly, or by role play?

    v. Mastery Checking

       of individual pairs – how many checkers available?

    vi. Extra Coaching

        for those in need – how many coaches available?

    vii. Organization

        briefing about organizational issues, contact, records, etc.

    viii. Contracting – in some/all cases?

I: Process Monitoring

1. Self-referral

    ○ by helper or helped – to whom?
    ○ how available is "expert" help?
    ○ what sort/size of problems to be referred?

2. Self-recording

    ○ by helper or helped or both?
    ○ for every session or less frequently?
    ○ positive and negative aspects, or just positive?
    ○ what criteria and/or vocabulary?
    ○ checking records – who, when, where, how often?

3. Peer discussion

    o group or individual?
    o helpers and helped separate or together?
    o frequency and duration of review meetings?

4. Direct Observation

    o by far the most revealing!
    o checklist of criteria/desired behavior to hand?
    o by project coordinator or spare helper or other?
    o video or audio-tape for feedback purposes?

5. Coaching by supervisory staff

    o Observe
    o Observe + jointly intervene with assessor
    o Intervene to show assessor what is required
    o Return later to check performance

6. What for early and late finishers?
7. Reliability/validity moderated by supervising teachers?
8. Project Process

    o what checks on organizational aspects?
    o frequency/duration of review meetings between
       professionals?
    o need/procedures for minimizing noise or movement levels?
    o what other adjustment/modifications are needed?

9. Recognition of Successful Students

    immediate celebration/recognition for following/succeeding
    with the PAL strategy

10. Need to watch for cheating or other fraud?

J: Formative Assessment of Continuous Student Progress

1. Examine the quality of peer feedback now and over time
2. Over time, moderate reliability and validity of feedback
3. Feedback this information to students
4. Direct observation by the teacher of learning outcomes.
5. What social, communicative transferable skills observed/
   measured?

(continued)

(continued)

6. Teacher checks on student self-recorded evidence of progress through materials
7. Teacher checks peer-administered tests or probes integral to helping procedure
8. Teacher curriculum based measurement

    (generalization tasks, probes, mini-tests delivered and scored by the teacher)

9. Computer assisted curriculum based assessment

    (delivered or/and scored by computer)

10. Computer assisted norm-referenced adaptive assessment

    (assessing generalization, delivered or/and scored by computer, preferably items selected randomly from large item bank on each occasion, can be used frequently without large practice effects)

11. Extrinsic or intrinsic rewards?

K: Evaluation (Summative)

1. Purpose of the Evaluation

    if there's no purpose, don't do it!

2. Peer Assisted Evaluation

    How can you engage students in the evaluation process?

3. Current Assessment Practice

    extend to give time series data? (i.e. pre-project gains c.f. project gains)

4. Research Design
    - pre-post/baseline/comparison group/etc?
    - separate measures for helpers/helped?

5. Normative Testing
    - standardized tests assessing generalization to compare with "normal" expectation?
    - or before and after (pre- and post-test)?
    - computer assisted? (delivered or/and scored by computer),

6. Criterion-Referenced Testing

    ○ mastery testing to see if specific tasks/skills/information learnt – gives better results!
    ○ error frequency counts, materials mastered, increased speed, etc?

7. Individual vs. Group Testing

    ○ the quick and unreliable vs. the slow but detailed
    ○ individual testing on small sample?

8. Attitudinal Data

    ○ from individual or group interview/discussion?
    ○ from questionnaires, checklists, ratings?
    ○ other observers' subjective reaction?

9. Social Gains

    ○ improved relations or behavior?
    ○ how to measure? checklists, sociometry, disciplinary referrals?

10. Self-report Data

    analyze and relate to other outcomes

11. Other Process Data

    attendance, mean session length, observation checklists, etc.

12. Spin-off

    ○ observations of unpredicted side effects – positive and negative!
    ○ generalization to other participants, times, materials, subject areas, etc.
    ○ generalization to state or national test or examination results, etc.

13. Follow-up

    short- and long-term follow-up data highly desirable

(continued)

(continued)

L: Feedback

1. Collation of Information

   - who co-ordinates this?
   - how variously for different consumers?

2. Data Analysis

   - how to summarize?
   - what balance of verbal/numerical/graphic?
   - analysis of statistical significance? educational significance?

3. Feedback to Participants

   - group or individual?
   - helpers/helped separate or together?
   - verbal/written/audio-visual?

4. Feedback from Participants

   - group or individual?
   - verbal or written?
   - any suggestions for improvement?

5. Further Contracting

   - continue peer assessment/stop/reduce frequency?
   - change peer assessment method?
   - change peer assessment technique?
   - change subject area?
   - change pairings?
   - change organization?

6. Accolades/Recognition

   - assessors and/or assessees?
   - public commendation?
   - academic credit?
   - certificates, badges, etc.?

4

Theory and Evidence on Peer Assessment

Useful things can certainly be learned from some study of theory – as you will see.

Theory

A number of researchers have conducted work that has strong implications for building theories of peer learning (e.g., Chi, Siler, Jeong, Yamauchi, & Hausmann, 2001; King, 1998; Sluijsmans, Dochy, & Moerkerke, 1998). I have developed a model of peer assessment that incorporates several theoretical perspectives (Figure 4.1). This theoretical model applies not just to peer assessment, but to all forms of peer assisted learning.

The model includes a balance of Piagetian and Vygotskian perspectives, and acknowledges the roles of affect and communication. It also includes sub-processes of organization and engagement. These processes are synthesized by the learners to enhance understanding. Actual performance of peer assessment involves practice, leading to consolidation and enhanced performance. An inherently increased quantity of feedback of greater immediacy adds power to this effect. Beyond this, self-monitoring and self-regulation come increasingly into play, developing into fully explicit metacognition. The learners become more able to engage in deep learning.

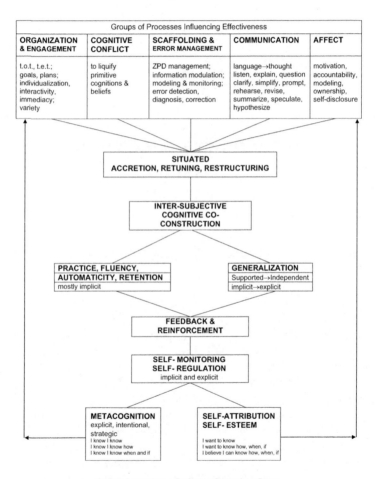

Figure 4.1 Theoretical Model of Peer Assessment

Organization and Engagement

The model initially divides some of the main sub-processes of peer assessment into five categories. The first of these includes organizational or structural features of the learning interaction, such as the need and press inherent in peer assessment toward increased time apparently looking at the task and maybe thinking about it (time on task) and time observably involved in doing something active leading to task completion (time engaged with task) – the two being different concepts. The need for both helper and helped to elaborate goals and plans, the individualization of learning and immediacy of feedback possible within the small group or one-on-one situation, and the variety of a novel kind of learning interaction are also included in this category.

Cognitive Conflict

This category encompasses the Piagetian school of thought (e.g., Piaget, 1926). It concerns the need to loosen cognitive blockages formed from old myths and false beliefs by presenting conflict and challenge via one or more peers. Teachers focus on learning as if the pupil was a blank slate. But, in fact, the pupil's head is full of all kinds of stuff, much of it factually or conceptually erroneous. So unlearning wrong stuff is as important as learning new stuff. Peers can be good at rooting out misconceptions in their partner – they certainly have more time for it than the teacher does.

Scaffolding and Error Management

By contrast, Vygotskian theory speaks of support and scaffolding from a more competent other, necessitating management of activities to be within the zone of proximal development of both parties in order to avoid any damaging excess of challenge (Vygotsky, 1978). The helper seeks to manage and modulate the information processing demands upon the learner – neither too much nor too little – to maximize the rate of progress. The helper also provides a cognitive model of competent performance.

The cognitive demands upon the helper in terms of monitoring learner performance and detecting, diagnosing, correcting and otherwise managing misconceptions and errors are great. Herein lies much of the cognitive exercise and benefit for the helper.

The greater the differential in ability or experience between the helper and the helped, the less cognitive conflict and the more scaffolding might be expected. Too great a differential might result in minimal cognitive engagement (let alone conflict) for the helper and unthinking but encapsulated acceptance with no re-tuning or co-construction by the helped. Of course, if the helper is older, more experienced, and therefore more credible but actually has no greater correct knowledge or ability than the helped, then a mismatch and faulty learning might occur in a different way.

Communication

Peer assessment also makes heavy demands upon the communication skills of both helper and helped, and in so doing can develop those skills. All participants might never have truly grasped a concept until they had to explain it to another, embodying and crystallizing thought into language – another Vygotskian idea, of course. Listening, explaining, questioning, summarizing, speculating, and hypothesizing are all valuable skills of effective peer assessment, which should be transferable to other contexts.

Affect

The affective component of peer assessment is also very powerful. A trusting relationship with a peer who holds no position of authority might facilitate self-disclosure of ignorance and misconception, enabling subsequent diagnosis and correction that could not occur otherwise. Modeling of enthusiasm and competence and belief in the possibility of success by the helper can influence the self-confidence of the helped, while a sense of loyalty and accountability to each other can help to keep the pair motivated and on-task.

Accretion, Re-tuning, Structuring, Inter-subjectivity

The five categories or sub-processes of level one (above) feed into a larger onward process in level two of extending each other's declarative knowledge, procedural skill and conditional and selective application of knowledge and skills by adding to and extending current capabilities (accretion), modifying current capabilities (re-tuning), and, in areas of completely new learning or cases of gross misconception or error, rebuilding new understanding (restructuring). These are somewhat similar to the Piagetian concepts of assimilation and accommodation. This leads in level three to the joint construction of a shared understanding between helper and helped which is adapted to the idiosyncrasies in their perceptions (i.e., is inter-subjective), is firmly situated within the current authentic context of application, and forms a foundation for further progress.

Practice and Generalization

As a result of the processes in the first three levels of Figure 4.1, peer assessment enables and facilitates a greater volume of engaged and successful practice, leading to consolidation, fluency and automaticity of thinking, and social, communicative and other core skills (level four). Much of this might occur implicitly, i.e., without the helper or helped being fully aware of what is happening with them. Simultaneously or subsequently, peer assessment can lead to generalization from the specific example in which a concept is learned, extending the ability to apply that concept to an ever-widening range of alternative and varied contexts.

Reinforcement

As some or all of the processes in the first three levels occur, both helper and helped give feedback to each other, implicitly and/or explicitly (level five). Indeed, implicit feedback is likely to have already occurred spontaneously in the earlier levels. Peer assessment increases the quantity and immediacy of feedback to the learner very substantially. Explicit reinforcement might stem from within the partnership or beyond it, by way of verbal and/or non-verbal praise, social acknowledgement and status, official accreditation, or even more tangible reward. However, reinforcement should not be indiscriminate or predominantly focused on effort.

Metacognition, Self-regulation, and Self-efficacy

As the learning relationship develops, both helper and helped should become more consciously aware of what is happening in their learning interaction, and more able to monitor and regulate the effectiveness of their own learning strategies in different contexts (level six). Development into fully conscious explicit and strategic metacognition (level seven) not only promotes more effective onward learning, it should make the helper and the helped more confident that they can achieve even more, and that their success is the result of their own efforts. In other words, they attribute success to themselves, not external factors, and their self-efficacy is heightened.

Levels of Learning

As the peer assessment relationship develops, the model continues to apply as the learning moves from the shallow, instrumental, surface level to the strategic level and on to the deep level as the students pursue their own goals rather than merely those set for them. Similarly, learning proceeds from the declarative (statements of existing fact) into the procedural (indicating how a situation developed and came to be) and conditional (suggesting what other alternatives might have been possible) (level eight). These affective and cognitive outcomes feed back into the originating five sub-processes – a continuous, iterative process.

Of course, it is unlikely that peer assessment in practice will neatly follow these levels or stages. Some may be missing (and the teacher can prompt for their insertion). Sometimes one level will occur before another which appears to follow it in the model. Most likely a number of events will occur that seem to be combinations of items in a level or across levels. Even where students work through to level eight, they may begin again at the outset or later on, usually but not always in relation to a new or varied task.

Evidence

The review below is initially based on existing reviews of the literature. However, much of the literature on peer assessment in concerned with students in university or college, and rather less with students in K-12 schools. This reflects the ease of access to their own students by university academics for research purposes. Schools can be elementary or secondary, and the organizational differences between these are such that implementation can be very different between the two environments. Consequently, I will take the two kinds of school separately, and discuss some individual papers as well as reviews.

The literature mostly focuses on typical students, but a few papers focus upon students with special needs or various kinds of disability; these will be noted. For this review the literature was newly searched, with a particular focus on 1998 through 2017, although occasionally earlier classic items have been included. The literature before this has already been searched and the results reported in O'Donnell and Topping (1998).

For the current chapter, four databases were searched: ERIC, Science Direct, Scopus, and ZETOC. The search terms were "peer assessment" AND school. Some 250 papers were retrieved initially. Qualitative, quantitative, and mixed methods studies were included, but qualitative studies only where the methodology for data analysis was clearly explicated. Some retrieved items concerned irrelevant groups, and some lacked any kind of data. This led to a final group of 6 reviews, 19 elementary studies and 21 high school studies.

Literature Reviews

An early review by Kane and Lawler (1978) considered research on three methods of peer assessment: peer nomination, peer rating, and peer ranking, noting that peer assessment could be reliable and valid. Peer nomination appeared to have the highest validity and reliability. Peer rating was the most useful of the three methods for feedback purposes.

A systematic literature review on the effects of peer assessment was reported by Van Gennip, Segers, and Tillema (2009). Fifteen studies since 1990 dealt with effects on achievement. However, only one of these studies included students from a school (a secondary school), the remainder consisting of university students. Peer assessment had positive effects. The authors developed four underlying constructs: psychological safety, value diversity, interdependence, and trust. Psychological safety was defined as a belief that it is safe to take interpersonal risks in a group of people or the extent of confidence in the rest of the group. Value diversity refers to differences in opinion about what a team's task, goal or mission should be – it should be low for peer work to be effective. Interdependence has been long studied, but needs to be perceived by the participants rather than assumed by teaching staff. It requires that multiple perspectives are made explicit and students are individually responsible for an active contribution to group discussions. In respect of trust, several studies noted that students feel uncomfortable criticizing one another's work, or found it difficult to rate their peers, at least initially.

A review of research on the role of peer assessment in the elementary science classroom was undertaken by Hodgson (2010). The themes that emerged consistently were the need for a supportive classroom climate, the role of talk and discussion that was not all teacher-led, the importance of questioning in the process, and the richness of feedback.

Tillema, Leenknecht, and Segers (2011) considered what quality criteria were specifically relevant to peer assessment. One hundred and thirty-two studies of peer assessment were selected, together with 42 studies for a qualitative analysis. Nowhere was any distinction made between studies based in school, higher education or other settings. Studies were evaluated with regard to two quality criteria: (1) the recognition of educational measurement criteria, and (2) the consideration of student involvement in the assessment of learning. Where emphasis was placed on authenticity and future learning needs across the lifespan, peer assessment had much to recommend it in terms of generalizability, particularly utility in contexts beyond the present institution.

Hoogeveen and van Gelderen (2013) were the only authors to mainly consider school students, in analyzing 26 studies of peer response on writing proficiency. They noted that several meta-studies had indicated that peer response was effective, but had not explored why. Many studies appeared to combine instruction in strategies, rules for interaction, and/or genre knowledge – and this seemed to be effective compared to individual writing.

Li et al. (2016) meta-analyzed studies on peer assessment in digital platforms mainly in universities since 1999, finding an average correlation between peer and teacher ratings of 0.63 – moderately strong. This correlation was higher when: (a) the peer assessment was paper-based rather than computer-assisted; (b) the subject area was not medical/clinical; (c) the course was graduate level rather than undergraduate or K-12; (d) individual work instead of group work was assessed; (e) the assessors and assessees were matched at random; (f) the peer assessment was voluntary instead of compulsory; (g) the peer assessment was non-anonymous; (h) peer raters provided both scores and qualitative comments instead of only scores; and (i) peer raters were involved in developing the rating criteria.

Now let us look at individual papers of interest with respect to elementary and high schools.

Elementary (Primary) Schools

Surveys

Weaver (1995) surveyed 500 teachers regarding the writing process. These teachers generally found peer responses to be more effective than their own. In contrast, students stated they found the teacher's responses to be more helpful in all stages of writing, but they nevertheless improved when they received peer feedback about their writing.

Atkinson (2003) conducted two surveys about assessment across the curriculum in Scotland, where formative assessment had been used in primary classrooms for many years, with the same class of students and their parents. A mix of formal and informal assessment and self- and peer assessment were valued. Parents did not want just summative assessment.

Bryant and Carless (2010) conducted extensive interviews and classroom observations in a two-year case study of Hong Kong classrooms, which tended to be dominated by repetitive learning and many high stakes tests. Student perceptions of the usefulness of peer assessment varied according to the quality of peer feedback, peer language proficiency, and the novelty or repetitiveness of its processes. Teachers and students viewed peer assessment as having longer-term applications.

Panadero and Brown (2017) conducted a survey of over 1500 primary, secondary, and higher education teachers in Spain to elicit their beliefs and values around peer assessment. Teachers reported occasional use of peer assessment in their classrooms but positive experience of it. The vast majority did not use anonymous forms of peer assessment and half of the teachers considered the students were accurate when assessing peers. The self-reported frequency of using peer assessment was strongly predicted by positive reasons for using peer assessment (rather than negative obstacles for avoiding it), prior use, beliefs that students should participate in assessment, and a willingness to include peer assessment in grading.

Non-traditional Subjects

Lin, Yang, Hung, and Wang (2006) reported the use of a web-based portfolio for appreciation and peer assessment for visual-art education in elementary school. Questionnaires and interviews were deployed and showed that the portfolio system could help student learning. The peer assessment component could help the students' learning in visual-art education. The web-based portfolios could help teachers to assess student learning progress and facilitate peer assessment.

Valle, Andrade, Palma, and Hefferen (2016) noted that feedback is crucial to students' growth as musicians. Fortunately, the teacher is not the sole source of feedback in the music classroom. Under the right conditions, students can provide actionable feedback to themselves and each other. This study showcased the work of three elementary music specialists who had innovatively incorporated formative peer assessment and self-assessment in their music lessons at grades 3 and 4 to promote student learning and self-direction.

Effectiveness

Harrison, O'Hara, and McNamara (2015) found that teacher assessment worked against the development of students into self-reliant people. Self- and peer-assessment were used with 523 students and their teachers. During self- and peer-assessment, students developed skills as critical, creative thinkers, effective communicators and collaborative team workers, becoming more personally productive and effective. Their self-awareness and self-reflection increased significantly. All of these were essential components of self-control and self-direction.

Buon (2016) studied children's uptake of feedback during peer assessment in primary school writing. Findings showed that pupils made better use of feedback if: it was task-involving and useful; there was sufficient time given for them to act on it and discuss it with their peers; and they were asked to reflect on how it had been used to improve the quality of the assessed work.

Yu and Wu (2016) sought to examine the individual and combined predictive effects of the quality of online peer feedback provided and received on primary school students' quality of question-generation. Performance data from 213 grade 5 students engaged in online question-generation and peer assessment for six weeks were analyzed. Results indicated that the quality of peer feedback provided and received predicted students' quality of question-generation.

Efficacy of Different Modes of Presentation

Two studies examined the efficacy of different methods of applying peer assessment in elementary schools. Yang, Ko, and Chung (2005) developed a web-based interactive writing environment in a two-year longitudinal study. Peer assessment was used to provide constructive comments to foster students' ability to review and criticize other writers' essays, to enable students to review their own essay, and to encourage students to improve their writing skills. Students who participated in the writing environment submitted many essays, interacted with other students online, and reviewed other essays, improving their writing skills.

By contrast, Chin and Teou (2009) used concept cartoons with two parallel experimental classes of younger (9–10-year-old) and older (10–11-year-old) students. The cartoons presented opposing viewpoints about scientific ideas to stimulate talk and argumentation among students in small peer assessment groups. The dialogic talk and interactive argumentation of the students provided diagnostic feedback about students' misconceptions about scientific principles to the teacher, and was helpful in moving students towards better understanding.

Gender Effects

Yurdabakan (2011) conducted a study in a primary school grade 4 social sciences course with 46 participants (28 female and 18 male), their ages ranging from 9 to 10. Students scored their same and opposite sexes with respect to their contribution to group work and their learning levels. The compatibility between female student and teacher scores was higher than male student and teacher scores (the teacher was male).

Social Aspects

Studies using measures of academic achievement have found that students who score high on these are more accepted, less rejected and disliked by peers, viewed by teachers as less deviant, and engage in more positive interactions than those who score low on achievement (e.g., Malecki & Elliott, 2002). This may suggest that able students would make the best peer assessors. However, Bryan's (2005) research demonstrated that certain types of social skills interventions (particularly those focused on self-perceptions, self-attributions, and locus of control) had consistent positive effects on academic achievement. The implication of this is that by engaging *all* students in peer assessment, it should be possible to raise the self-esteem and social-connectedness of rejected children and raise their academic achievement.

Frederickson and Furnham (2004) compared behavioral characteristics assessed by 867 typical classmates in mainstream middle schools (8–12-years-old) for children with moderate learning difficulties (MLD) (*n* = 32) and socially rejected but not-MLD children (*n* = 38), and their typical classmates (*n* = 287). Systematic differences were identified between MLD and typical students in the peer-assessed behavioral characteristics, while there were no differences between typical and socially rejected students.

Four methods of assessing children's friendships were compared by Yugar and Shapiro (2001), addressing peer nominations (naming children you were friendly with), peer ratings (ranking children you were friendly with), and reciprocal peer nominations (naming children you were friendly with when they also named you). There was high agreement between reciprocal peer nominations and peer ratings, but regular peer nominations did not appear to be reliable. The extent to which social affiliation should be regarded as important when matching for peer assessment is an interesting one. Many practitioners do not match students who are already highly socially affiliated (since they may enjoy their relationship rather than using it to facilitate achievement), but also tend not match students who are strongly negatively affiliated.

Students with Special Needs

Peer assessment has been used successfully with special needs children (e.g., Scruggs & Mastropieri, 1998), with students as young as grade 4 (nine years old). Importantly, there are gains from functioning as either assessor or assessee. Studies in this category also have implications for matching students involved in peer assessment. O'Keefe (1991) examined sociometric surveys and peer assessments of social behavior in 51 grade 3 through 6 mainstream classrooms in order to identify accepted and rejected intellectually challenged and non-challenged children. Rejected intellectually challenged children were perceived by their peers as aggressive/disruptive and/or sensitive/isolated. In contrast, accepted intellectually challenged children were perceived as sociable. The same relationships were found for typical children. This is encouraging, since it suggests that special needs status is no prohibition for involvement in peer assessment, although disruptive or isolated behavior might be.

Similarly, Rockhill and Asher (1992) examined gender differences in the types of behavior that distinguished between low-accepted children and their better-accepted classmates. Third- through fifth-graders ($n = 881$) in five elementary schools completed a sociometric scale and a peer nomination measure. The same behaviors were important for boys and girls. Both aggressive and withdrawn low-accepted children received lower peer ratings for prosocial behavior. Children seemed to be blind to the condition or label of the problem individuals and took their behavior at face value. This is encouraging, though the effect may diminish as children grow older.

High (Secondary) School

High schools are more complex environments than elementary schools, and what works in the latter may not work in the former.

Perceived Value of Peer Assessment

Black and Harrison (2001) documented case studies of 12 teachers in six schools and reported some concern about whether peer assessment was practicable. Cultural differences were noted by Mok (2011), using interviews and classroom observation to report on moves towards peer assessment in the test-oriented special region of Hong Kong. Peer assessment has been recognized as enhancing student learning if sensitively implemented (Sebba, Crick, Yu, Lawson, Harlen, & Durant, 2008).

Accuracy of Peer Assessment

In Taiwan, Sung, Chang, Chiou, and Hou (2005) used progressively focused self- and peer assessment procedures with students developing designs for new websites. Two classes of 76 14–15-year-olds of above average ability assessed random websites produced by their colleagues. Self-assessment preceded peer assessment. The quality of the students' performance improved after the peer assessment activities. Similarly, Tseng and Tsai (2007) found that peer assessment scores were highly correlated with teacher scores.

Tsivitanidou, Zacharia, and Hovardas (2011) investigated secondary school students' peer assessment skills in Greece. Two classes of seventh graders (age 14, $n = 36$, gender balanced) were anonymously assigned to reciprocally assess their peers' science web-portfolios. Interviews, video observation, and peer assessors' feedback found that the students had positive attitudes towards peer assessment and that they intend to implement it again.

Chang, Tseng, Chou, and Chen (2011) examined the reliability and validity of web-based portfolio peer assessment with 72 15–16-year-old students taking a computer course in a senior high school. Peer assessment scores were not consistent with teacher assessment scores and significant differences were found between peer assessment scores and end-of-course examination scores. The quality of training in peer assessment for these students was questionable and no assessment rubric was negotiated with the students.

Effectiveness of Peer Assessment

The study by Sung et al. (2005) suggested that not only were students' peer assessments consistent with the assessments of teachers, but the quality of the students' work in developing new websites improved after the peer assessment activities as well. Similarly, Tseng and Tsai (2007) found that 184 tenth grade 16-year-old students significantly improved their projects for a computer course by engaging in successive rounds of peer assessment activities. The study also related the type of peer assessment feedback (reinforcing, didactic, corrective or suggestive) to subsequent performance in the student projects. Reinforcing peer feedback was useful in the development of better projects. Suggestive feedback was helpful in the beginning of peer assessment. However, didactic feedback, and to an extent corrective feedback, were negatively correlated with student achievement.

Crane and Winterbottom (2008) investigated how peer assessment could help students to learn about photosynthesis in a "high attaining" Year Nine class in a UK 11–18 comprehensive school. A conceptually demanding topic like photosynthesis provided an excellent context to examine how peer assessment could impact on the learning of high attaining students, an area where research is limited. Analysis of data derived from questionnaires, individual interviews and conventional tests suggested that: (1) a six-week multi-component peer assessment intervention can have an impact on students' learning, and (2) some of the effect on learning may be linked to the way in which peer assessment enhanced students' own understanding of the role they played in their learning, and hence their autonomy in learning.

Chang and Tseng (2009) conducted a study in Taiwan on the use of peer assessment of web-based portfolios and its effect on student performance with 13–14-year-olds in two computer classes of 30 students each (one class intervention, the other control). There was no significant difference between groups in academic achievement and computer achievement. Chang and Chou (2011) examined the effects of reflection quality in peer assessment on learning outcomes with 45 14-year-old students during a web-based portfolio process. The immediate influence of reflection quality on learning outcomes was small, but positive and statistically significant. Follow-up contrasts found reflection quality significantly related to an achievement test, work, and attitude outcomes.

A Belgian team (Gielen, Peeters, Dochy, Onghena, & Struyven, 2010) examined the effectiveness of certain characteristics of peer assessment feedback in a quasi-experimental, repeated measures study of 43 13-year-old students. Written assignments showed that receiving justified comments in feedback was related to improvements in writing performance, but this effect diminished for students with higher pre-test performance. The effect of accuracy of feedback was less than the effect of justification.

Sung, Chang, Chang, and Yu (2010) explored peer assessment in individual music performance with 116 seventh graders. Then 110 eighth graders had student-constructed web pages subject to peer assessments. Reliability and validity increased with the number of raters in both studies. Low- and high-achieving students tended to over- and underestimate the quality of their work, respectively. The discrepancy between the ratings of students and experts was higher in group-work assessments than in individual-work assessments.

Chang and Wu (2012) explored the reliability and validity of assessment under a web-based portfolio assessment environment. Participants were 72 eleventh graders taking a "Computer Applications" course. The students performed portfolio creation, inspection, self- and peer-assessment using the web-based portfolio assessment system. Meanwhile, the teachers used the assessment tool to review students' portfolios and evaluate their learning performances. The results indicated that the portfolio scores were highly consistent with students' end-of-course examination scores, implying that web-based portfolio assessment is a valid assessment method.

Lu and Law (2012) studied 181 high school students engaged in online peer assessment. Peers graded and gave feedback, which was analyzed. Lu and Law found that the provision by student assessors of feedback that identified problems and gave suggestions was a significant predictor of the performance of the assessors themselves, and that positive affective feedback was related to the performance of assessees.

Van Zundert, Sluijsmans, Konings, and van Merrienboer (2012) had 110 secondary school students that studied four integrated tasks, requiring them to learn a domain-specific skill and how to assess a fictitious peer performing the same skill. Additionally, the students performed two domain-specific test tasks and two peer assessment test tasks. Peer assessment skills were superposed on domain-specific skills and therefore suffered more when higher cognitive load was induced by increased task complexity.

Hovardas, Tsivitanidou, and Zahcharias (2014) had 28 seventh graders anonymously assess each other's science web-portfolios. Peer assessors and an expert assessor used the same pre-specified assessment criteria. Peer assessees received feedback from two peers and the expert. Quantitative feedback differed between peer assessors and the expert and also between peer assessors – reliability was low. However, qualitative feedback was similar in that both included the structural components of written feedback. The majority of changes proposed by peer assessors were scientifically accurate.

Chetcuti and Cutajar (2014) explored the implementation of peer assessment with a group of students studying advanced physics in a secondary school. The study investigated how the views of students regarding peer assessment evolved as they engaged with peer assessment. The students were formerly very much immersed in a traditional assessment culture and needed to be trained to develop peer assessment skills. Student concerns related to fairness and their abilities as assessors. Dependence on the teacher as "expert" remained unchanged as the students engaged with peer assessment. Successful implementation of peer assessment requires a re-examination of the roles of student and teachers as assessors within a safe learning environment.

Hsia, Huang, and Hwang (2016) used a web-based peer-assessment method for performing arts activities. This was applied to 163 junior high students (experimental group and control group). A control group learned with a web-based streaming video-supported environment. Peer assessment using a rubric significantly improved the students' performance, self-efficacy and motivation. Peer assessment ratings were highly correlated with teachers' ratings on every performance item. Performance ratings were highly related to the students' self-efficacy. Students who learned with peer assessment were significantly more satisfied with the learning activity than controls.

Hsu (2016) used a peer assessment system involving a grid-based knowledge classification approach to improve students' performance during computer skills training. The participants were divided into three groups: one that learned with traditional instruction, one given conventional peer assessment, and one using the grid-based peer assessment system. The results showed that the learning achievements of the students using the grid-based system were significantly better than those of the other two groups.

Scott (2017) used a "simulated" peer-assessment activity to improve performance in numerical problem-solving questions in high school biology. The benefits of using "simulated," rather than real, student answers in peer assessment was discussed. Student improvement in performance and attitude towards the activity was measured. The results suggested that "simulated" peer assessment is suitable as a replacement for regular peer assessment and that student attitudes favor the simulated approach.

Summary

Reviews

Six reviews of varying quality and varying degrees of focus solely upon schools generally found peer assessment effective in raising and deepening attainment. Psychological safety and trust were emphasized, as well as the importance of a supportive classroom climate. In writing, instruction in strategies, rules for interaction and genre knowledge seemed important features to embed in peer assessment. The most recent review emphasized that there was high correlation between teacher and peer assessments. Involving peer assessors in developing the assessment criteria, enabling them to provide qualitative comments rather than just scores, and making peer assessment voluntary and non-anonymous, were all associated with higher effectiveness.

Primary Schools

There were 19 elementary school studies selected. Four surveys of teacher use of peer assessment were reported. Generally teachers in the West thought peer assessment effective but did not use it all that much. However, in the East the picture was more mixed, given the prevailing classroom culture. Peer assessment was reported in non-traditional subjects such as music and visual arts. There were three studies of effectiveness, all of them with positive results. Two studies investigated different methods of presenting peer assessment, one concerned with peer assessment in a web environment and one exploring the use of concept cartoons. Both yielded positive results. In the only study of gender effects girls' peer assessments were found to be closer to the teachers than were those of boys. Regarding social aspects, training can increase the ability of students to participate in peer assessment. Peer assessment of behavioral characteristics shows children do not discriminate between normal and socially rejected children, but they do with respect to children with moderate learning disability. Practitioners tend to avoid matching high or low socially affiliated children with each other for peer assessment. Children with Special Needs/Disability have been successfully involved in peer assessment. Aggressive/disruptive or socially isolated children might be difficult to match successfully.

Secondary Schools

There were 21 secondary studies selected. Peer assessment was not necessarily seen as practicable almost 20 years ago, and there are still concerns about cultural acceptability in the East. However, more recently in the West it has been widely accepted. Four studies looked at accuracy of peer assessment. Three of these found positive results, but the fourth found peer assessment did not correlate with teacher assessment of examination results – although there was no training or involvement of the students in developing assessment criteria. Fifteen studies of effectiveness follow. All of these except one reported positive results. This included several studies deploying peer assessment in a technological environment. Qualitative feedback might be more reliable than quantitative feedback. Giving justification of reasons for feedback improves outcomes. If task complexity increases, quality of peer assessment may suffer. Studies in music and visual arts showed positive results. One successful study was with high attaining students.

The next chapter goes from considering the background theory and evidence on peer assessment to describing how you might evaluate your own peer assessment project.

References

Atkinson, P. (2003). *Assessment 5–14: What do pupils and parents think?* Spotlight. Education Resources Information Center document reproduction service ED480897.

Black, P., & Harrison, C. (2001). Self- and peer-assessment and taking responsibility: The science student's role in formative assessment. *School Science Review, 83*(302), 43–49.

Boon, S. I. (2016). Increasing the uptake of peer feedback in primary school writing: Findings from an action research enquiry. *Education 3–13, 44*(2), 212–225.

Bryan, T. (2005). Science-based advances in the social domain of learning disabilities. *Learning Disability Quarterly, 28*, 119–121.

Bryant, D. A., & Carless, D. R. (2010). Peer assessment in a test-dominated setting: Empowering, boring or facilitating examination preparation? *Educational Research for Policy and Practice, 9*(1), 3–15.

Chang, C. C., & Tseng, K. H. (2009). Use and performances of web-based portfolio assessment. *British Journal of Educational Technology, 40*(2), 358–370.

Chang, C. C., & Chou, P. N. (2011). Effects of reflection category and reflection quality on learning outcomes during web-based portfolio assessment process: A case study of high school students in computer application course. *Turkish Online Journal of Educational Technology, 10*(3), 101–114.

Chang, C. C., & Wu, B. H. (2012). Is teacher assessment reliable or valid for high school students under a web-based portfolio environment? *Educational Technology & Society, 15*(4), 265–278.

Chang, C. C., Tseng, K. H., Chou, P. N., & Chen, Y. H. (2011). Reliability and validity of web-based portfolio peer assessment: A case study for a senior high school's students taking computer course. *Computers and Education, 57*(1), 1306–1316.

Chetcuti, D., & Cutajar, C. (2014). Implementing peer assessment in a post-secondary (16–18) physics classroom. *International Journal of Science Education, 36*(18), 3101–3124.

Chi, M. T. H., Siler, S. A., Jeong, H., Yamauchi, T., & Hausmann, R. G. (2001). Learning from human tutoring. *Cognitive Science, 25*, 471–533.

Chin, C., & Teou, L. Y. (2009). Using concept cartoons in formative assessment: Scaffolding students' argumentation. *International Journal of Science Education*, *31*(10), 1307–1332.

Crane, L., & Winterbottom, M. (2008). Plants and photosynthesis: Peer assessment to help students learn. *Journal of Biological Education*, *42*(4), 150–156.

Frederickson, N. L., & Furnham, A. E. (2004). Peer-assessed behavioural characteristics and sociometric rejection: Differences between pupils who have moderate learning difficulties and their mainstream peers. *British Journal of Educational Psychology*, *74*(3), 391–410.

Gielen, S., Peeters, E., Dochy, F., Onghena, P., & Struyven, K. (2010). Improving the effectiveness of peer feedback for learning. *Learning and Instruction*, *20*(4), 304–315.

Harrison, K., O'Hara, J., & McNamara, G. (2015). Re-thinking assessment: Self- and peer-assessment as drivers of self-direction in learning. *Eurasian Journal of Educational Research*, *60*, 75–88.

Hodgson, C. (2010). Assessment for learning in science: What works? *Primary Science*, *115*, 14–16.

Hoogeveen, M., & van Gelderen, A. (2013). What works in writing with peer response? A review of intervention studies with children and adolescents. *Educational Psychology Review*, *25*(4), 473–502. DOI: 10.1007/s10648-013-9229-z.

Hovardas, T., Tsivitanidou, O. E., & Zahcharias, C. Z. (2014). Peer versus expert feedback: An investigation of the quality of peer feedback among secondary school students. *Computers & Education*, *71*, 133–152.

Hsia, L. H., Huang, I., & Hwang, G. J. (2016). A web-based peer-assessment approach to improving junior high school students' performance, self-efficacy and motivation in performing arts courses. *British Journal of Educational Technology*, *47*(4), 618–632.

Hsu, T. C. (2016). Effects of a peer assessment system based on a grid-based knowledge classification approach on computer skills training. *Educational Technology & Society*, *19*(4), 100–111.

Kane, J. S., & Lawler, E. E. (1978). Methods of peer assessment. *Psychological Bulletin*, *85*(3), 555–586.

King, A. (1998). Transactive peer tutoring: Distributing cognition and metacognition. *Educational Psychology Review*, *10*(1), 57–74.

Li, H., Xiong, Y., Zang, X., Kornhaber, M. L., Lyu, Y., Chung, K. S., & Suen, H. K. (2016). Peer assessment in the digital age: A meta-analysis comparing peer and teacher ratings. *Assessment & Evaluation in Higher Education*, *41*(2), 245–264.

Lin, K. C., Yang, S. H., Hung, J. C., & Wang, D. M. (2006). Web-based appreciation and peer-assessment for visual-art education. *International Journal of Distance Education Technologies*, 4(4), 5–14.

Lu, J., & Law, N. (2012). Online peer assessment: Effects of cognitive and affective feedback. *Instructional Science*, 40(2), 257–275. DOI: 10.1007/s11251-011-9177-2

Malecki, C. K., & Elliott, C. N. (2002). Children's social behaviors as predictors of academic achievement: A longitudinal analysis. *School Psychology Quarterly*, 17, 1–23.

Mok, J. (2011). A case study of students' perceptions of peer assessment in Hong Kong. *ELT Journal*, 65(3), 230–239.

O'Donnell, A. M., & Topping, K. J. (1998). Peers assessing peers: Possibilities and problems. In: K. Topping & S. Ehly, *Peer-assisted learning*. Mahwah, NJ: Lawrence Erlbaum.

O'Keefe, P. F. (1991). *Relationship between social status and peer assessment of social behavior among mentally retarded and non-retarded children*. Educational Resources Information Centre document reproduction service ED340500.

Panadero, E., & Brown, G. T. L. (2017). Teachers' reasons for using peer assessment: Positive experience predicts use. *European Journal of Psychology of Education*, 32(1), 133–156.

Piaget, J. P. (1926). *The language and thought of the child*. London: Routledge & Kegan Paul.

Rockhill, C. M., & Asher, S. R. (1992). *Peer assessment of the behavioral characteristics of poorly accepted boys and girls*. Educational Resources Information Center document reproduction service ED346372.

Scott, F. J. (2017). A simulated peer-assessment approach to improve students' performance in numerical problem-solving questions in high school biology. *Journal of Biological Education*, 51(2), 107–122.

Scruggs, T. E., & Mastropieri, M. A. (1998). Tutoring and students with special needs. In: K. J. Topping & S. Ehly (Eds.), *Peer-assisted learning*. Mahwah, NJ: Lawrence Erlbaum.

Sebba, J., Crick, R. D., Yu, G., Lawson, H., Harlen, W., & Durant, K. (2008). *Systematic review of research evidence of the impact on students in secondary schools of self and peer assessment*. Technical report. In: *Research Evidence in Education Library*. London: EPPI-Centre, Social Science Research Unit, Institute of Education, University of London.

Sluijsmans, D., Dochy, F., & Moerkerke, G. (1998). Creating a learning environment by using self-, peer-, and co-assessment. *Learning Environments Research*, 1(3), 293–319.

Sung, Y. T., Chang, K. E., Chiou, S. K., & Hou, H. T. (2005). The design and application of a web-based self- and peer-assessment system. *Computers and Education*, 45(2), 187–202.

Sung, Y. T., Chang, K. E., Chang, T. H., & Yu, W. C. (2010). How many heads are better than one? The reliability and validity of teenagers' self- and peer assessments. *Journal of Adolescence*, 33(1), 135–145.

Tillema, H., Leenknecht, M., & Segers, M. (2011). Assessing assessment quality: Criteria for quality assurance in design of (peer) assessment for learning – A review of research studies. *Studies in Educational Evaluation*, 37(1), 25–34.

Tseng, S. C., & Tsai, C. C. (2007). On-line peer assessment and the role of the peer feedback: A study of high school computer course. *Computers and Education*, 49(4), 1161–1174.

Tsivitanidou, O. E., Zacharia, Z. C., & Hovardas, T. (2011). Investigating secondary school students' unmediated peer assessment skills. *Learning and Instruction*, 21(4), 506–519.

Valle, C., Andrade, H., Palma, M., & Hefferen, J. (2016). Applications of peer assessment and self-assessment in music. *Music Educators Journal*, 102(4), 41–49.

Van Gennip, N. A. E., Segers, M., & Tillema, H. M. (2009). Peer assessment for learning from a social perspective: The influence of interpersonal variables and structural features. *Educational Research Review*, 4(1), 41–54.

Van Zundert, M., Sluijsmans, D. M. A., Konings, K. D., & van Merrienboer, J. J. G. (2012). The differential effects of task complexity on domain-specific and peer assessment skills. *Educational Psychology*, 32(1), 127–145.

Vygotsky, L. S. (1978). *Mind in society: The development of higher psychological processes*. M. Cole, V. John-Steiner, S. Scribner, & E. Souberman (Eds.). Cambridge, MA: MIT Press.

Weaver, M. E. (1995). Using peer response in the classroom: Students' perspectives. *Research and Teaching in Developmental Education*, 12, 31–37.

Yang, J. C., Ko, H. W., & Chung, I. L. (2005). Web-based interactive writing environment: Development and evaluation. *Educational Technology and Society*, 8(2), 214–229.

Yu, F. Y., & Wu, C. P. (2016). Predictive effects of the quality of online peer-feedback provided and received on primary school students' quality of question-generation. *Educational Technology & Society*, *19*(3), 234–246.

Yugar, J. M., & Shapiro, E. S. (2001). Elementary children's school friendship: A comparison of peer assessment methodologies. *School Psychology Review*, *30*(4), 68–85.

Yurdabakan, I. (2011). The investigation of peer assessment in primary school cooperative learning groups with respect to gender. *Education 3–13*, *39*(2), 153–169.

5

Evaluating Peer Assessment

Just because spectacular results have been achieved with peer assessment in some places, it doesn't guarantee that you will get them. Especially with your first effort, you are likely to want to know how successful you have been, with a view to improving effectiveness even more in the future. And evaluating yourself is a lot more comfortable than some outsider doing it. Evaluation will also help convince your colleagues of the value of peer assessment, and encourage them to emulate your good work. Beyond that, it may be that your good works will disseminate to other schools, whereby you will indirectly have a profound effect on the education of a very large number of students.

Most importantly, you will find the helpers and helped students very eager to be told how they've done – so you'd better have something concrete to tell them! The helpers and helped will value their own feelings about how well they have done. However, you are the expert, so they will value your opinion on how well they have done even more. If all you have to give them is vague well-meaning platitudes, your credibility (and the program) is going to suffer.

Another major purpose of evaluation is reinforcement for yourself. A fuzzy feeling that the project "went OK" is unlikely to give you the confidence and reassurance you need to consolidate and develop your peer assessment initiative. If you have more concrete data about the success of the project, which is independent of your own subjective views, you will feel you are working from a more solid foundation. Also, if you can present scientific data on your effectiveness as a planner and coordinator of peer assessment projects, this is unlikely to do your promotion prospects any harm!

One of the great virtues of peer assessment is its cost-effectiveness, i.e. what the helpers and helped get out of it for the time and effort put in by professional teachers who are managing and coordinating the project. Thus it would be nonsensical for the professionals to spend a vast amount of their time evaluating a project. However, a small amount of time is probably worth devoting to this task. This chapter details some of the ways of going about it. You will need to choose the ways you think are best and easiest for your own situation.

Objectives

Before you can determine whether or not your project was a success, you need to be clear about why you did it in the first place. Project coordinators often have a wide range of objectives in mind when they embark on a particular initiative, but they do not always articulate these consciously. Program objectives should be specified at the outset – in a way which is measurable – in clear, precise, observable and operational terms. Don't make this list of objectives unrealistically long or over-ambitious, however, or you will just build in failure. Even with a modest number of objectives, you are unlikely to achieve them all – but you might find there are other serendipitous gains which you had not expected.

Remember that the program objectives espoused by the professional program coordinator may be quite different from those of the helpers, helped, or other relevant professional colleagues. Thus, while you may be out to raise attainment, the helped students may be out to have a good time, the helpers may be wanting to feel grandiose and powerful, while the school principal may be wanting the project to reduce conflict in the playground between two sets of pupils, and traditionalist colleagues may be wanting the project to fall apart at the seams to justify their conviction that such modern ideas are doomed to failure and the old ways are undoubtedly the best. Different stake-holders have different objectives, some spoken and some unspoken, and you are most unlikely to be able to meet all of them.

Types of Evaluation

There are two main types of evaluation: "Process" (or Formative) evaluation and "Product" (or Summative or Outcome) evaluation (similar to the two kinds of assessment). Summative or outcome evaluation looks solely at the end-product of a project, without looking closely at how effective each of the various aspects of the organization and methods of the project were in achieving this goal. These latter questions are the focus of formative evaluation, so named because the data gathered enable you to re-form a better project next time, or even adjust the current one as you go along.

A number of reports of projects in the literature include no data about outcomes, but merely constitute a description of how the project worked. While this kind of "evaluation" can give the project organizer a nice warm rosy glow, the "grateful testimonials" approach will be regarded with cynicism by many hard-headed professionals. The description itself needs to be precise. How many meetings were held, and what was the attendance rate by different categories of personnel? What was the participation rate of helpers and helped, as well as frequency and regularity of contacts made during the project? Was the desired behavior demonstrated by helpers, helped and project coordinators? Did the helpers actually implement the helping procedures in which they had been trained, or could the improvement shown by the helped students be attributed solely to the effect of extra individual attention? Did the project coordinator monitor sessions regularly and frequently as expected? Were learning materials prepared in good time and always brought to sessions? Was record keeping completed as required, and were all records subsequently collated for analysis?

The fundamental question with the process aspect of project evaluation is whether or not the project actually operated as planned and intended. This is known as "implementation integrity" or "implementation fidelity." Without process data, outcome data cannot be construed to reflect upon the effectiveness of the program. On the other hand, even a quantitative description of project process remains no more than that – it tells us whether the project was put into operation as intended, but does not tell us whether it "worked."

Research Design

Evaluation research is basically about detecting change and measuring the degree of change. The obvious thing is to apply your measure(s) at the start of the project and again at the end of the project to the students who take part (Pre-Post Test Design). But if your measure is not norm-referenced (standardized), you will have no way of telling whether the children would have made the pre-post changes anyway, irrespective of the project. (Standardization refers to averages for hundreds of children from all over the country.) Even if your measure is norm-referenced (like a standardized reading test), unless your results are spectacularly better than "normal" rates of gain, you still won't have proof that the children could only have made those gains with the help of the project.

However, the standardization may not be immediately relevant to a small group of children with peculiar attainment profiles in your particular educational establishment. So you really need to compare the progress of your project students with the progress of a similar local group that has not been involved in the project. If you offer involvement in the project to 20 students, but only ten finally participate, you can use the ten "drop-outs" as a "comparison" group.

But the ten drop-outs are not a true "control" group, because they have self-selected not to participate, and factors that incline them to do that are likely to be associated with the factors causing their difficulties. Nevertheless, it is better to have a comparison group than not, so you should apply your measure(s) pre- and post-project to both groups. Don't try to make out your comparison group is a control group, though.

To get a true control group, you would list your 20 children, then allocate them randomly to "control" or "intervention" groups (by tossing a coin or using random number tables). Both groups would be pre-tested, then only the "intervention" group invited to participate. However, not all of them might agree, so you would then have:

Control Group   Experimental Group
$n = 10$ Participating $n = 5$
                        Not participating $n = 5$

In any event, the numbers quoted here in the intervention sub-groups are so small as to make comparisons of doubtful validity. A minimum sample size of ten is desirable to begin to have any real confidence in your results.

There are alternative approaches, which can be nearly as "scientifically" acceptable and which can prove easier to do, especially where pre-existing data can be utilized. If for the students concerned there has been in the past a regular routine of applying attainment tests, historical data may be available for the project group. This enables you to scrutinize the fluctuations in progress in the past, and see how the gains during the project compare. This is called the (Interrupted) Time Series Design. Acceleration during the project should be fairly clearly evident in relation to previous rates of progress. Even better, and demanding little extra work, would be the inclusion of similar time series data from a comparison group.

As will already be evident, one of the problems with true control groups is that their use involves denying a service or facility to people who clearly seem to be in need of it. It can be argued that until you have demonstrated that the project has worked satisfactorily by using the control group, you don't actually know whether you are denying the control group anything worthwhile, but this logical contention does not tend to go down that well with caring teachers.

A design that is useful in getting round this problem is the Discontinuity Design. Where a limited amount of a service or facility is available, there is often felt to be a moral obligation that all those in greatest need receive the service. If enough service is available to meet the needs of those who are worst off, but still leave some spare capacity, the limited surplus service may be extended to the larger band of those whose needs are less severe. But how to allocate the limited surplus to this large group? Arguably, random selection for project inclusion is the fairest way to go about it for this mid-band of students. Then the performance of otherwise similar included and non-included students around the margin of selection can be compared.

Finally, one further design is probably worth mentioning, which also gets round the ethical problems involving using control groups. This is the Multiple Baseline Design. If a larger group of potential clients exists than can be serviced at one time, they may have to be serviced by two consecutive projects. Where one half of the clients have to be serviced first, and the second later, it is reasonable and fair to allocate to "early" and "late" groups randomly. The gains of the "early" group can be compared in the short run to the progress of the "late" group. Subsequently, variations in procedure can be applied to one or other group, and gains compared within and between groups.

Other, more complex, designs are also possible. Whatever you choose to do, some attempt to guard against the Hawthorne effect is necessary – the effect whereby the clients of an intervention show brief improvement purely because some attention is being paid to them and there is some element of novelty about the proceedings, quite irrespective of the actual nature of the intervention. Another possible source of embarrassment is the "John Henry effect" — where the control group, alerted to the fact that somebody considers them to be in need but is not providing anything for them, determines to improve anyway, and does so without apparent outside intervention.

Measures

Peer Assisted Evaluation

The first thing to remember is that you don't have to do all the work. It would be paradoxical to operate a peer assessment project and then resort to purely teacher-driven methods of evaluation. It is perfectly possible to have the participating students themselves collect data. Of course, you can gather their opinions. You might think of questionnaires, but also think about students interviewing each other. Can you have the students apply tests to each other as well? Remember, you can have the students score them. Maybe you can even have some students doing the data analysis as a special project. The project coordinator's time is limited, so decisions have to be made about how many and which evaluative measures are going to be applied to helper and helped respectively.

There are various basic requirements of any measures you seek to use. Economy of cost in materials and of time in administration and scoring are two obvious considerations. The measure needs to be reliable, in the sense of not being susceptible to wild, random fluctuations or erratic guesswork. It also needs to be valid, i.e. one must be assured that it actually measures what it is purporting to measure. Of equal importance, it needs to be relevant to the processes in question. Last, but by no means least, the measure must generate information that is analyzable. A vast quantity of impressionistic opinion may be fascinating to the project organizers, but will not enable them to communicate their findings to others in a clear and credible way.

Individual vs. Group Tests

The peer assessment experience is nothing if not personal. Problems tend to be solved jointly as much as individually, and help is more or less always at hand. The relationship and the speed of progress through the process is highly idiosyncratic. To attempt to assess the impact of an experience of this kind by the use of some sort of group test, wherein the students sit in isolation in serried ranks and wrestle without help with some alien task, seems logically to be something of a nonsense – or is it?

If you wish to determine whether peer assessment has improved abilities to function in a one-on-one situation, a measure administered to an individual personally would seem essential. But if you are anticipating that the experience will produce results that will spread and endure outside of the situation, then the application of a group test could be construed as a usefully stringent measure of generalization. However, remember that whatever the reliability of the group test quoted in the manual may be, with a small and idiosyncratically selected group of children with learning difficulties, reliability may be actually considerably less. Where group and individual tests have been used, correlation between the two kinds of test result might not be high. While the use of group tests may show substantial rates of gain taking in the project group as a whole, individual results may seem so implausible that they should not be given much weight.

Some peer assessment procedures incorporate peer-administered tests or probes. This is a form of peer-administered curriculum based measurement. The teacher might use some form of regular and frequent curriculum based measurement – generalization tasks, probes, mini-tests delivered and scored by the teacher. These data can be similarly cumulated over the course of a project and over all participants as part of a summative evaluation.

Norm-referenced vs. Criterion-referenced

Norm-referenced tests allow a student's performance to be compared with that of many others in various parts of the country. Criterion referenced tests allow a student's performance to be compared with his or her own previous performance or some other benchmark of performance relevant to the curriculum. The first compares the student with other students, and the second compares the student's performance with a pre-determined criterion of skill acquisition. All tests have inherent problems. They may provoke anxiety in some students, making their individual results largely meaningless. For others, the unreality and apparent purposelessness of the exercise produces equally strange results. What the test means to the student might be quite different to what it means for the teacher.

In elderly norm-referenced tests, the content is often dated and of doubtful interest to some specific student sub-groups. The standardization data may be neither recent nor localized, and the data on supposed reliability and validity may be based on very small numbers. The structure of the test may itself be problematic, and you may find in some cases that answering only one or two more questions correctly produces a substantial shift in standardized score – the briefer the test, the more likely it is to suffer from this problem.

In some cases, there may be grave doubts about the cross-reliability of supposedly "parallel" forms of the test. Some evaluators have tried to get round this by allocating different parallel forms at random to students at pre-test, and the remaining forms at random at post-test. Another problem is that standardized tests were not designed for repeated use in short time spans on a pre-post basis to evaluate relatively short projects – there might be "practice effects" from familiarity with the format of the test even if the content is different in parallel forms.

By contrast, the advantage of criterion-referenced tests is that they can much more flexibly reflect the reality of the peer assessment curriculum. Their disadvantage is that comparison with national norms is no longer possible, and the absence of that vast, distant quasi-"control" group means that much more emphasis must be placed on achieving an adequate evaluation design. Basically, a criterion-referenced test checks whether the helped students have learnt what they have been taught. While this may be simple and logical, such tests might not give information on how well the helped students can generalize new skills to other areas, unless this is built into the structure of the test. Nor may it be easy to obtain any idea of whether the student is accelerating at a rate that will eventually enable them to catch up with the average student.

Where a school is using a criterion-referenced measure of its own devising, it is worthwhile "piloting" it with a relevant local sub-group first. A check on the stability of the measure with a normal sample in the school on a test-re-test, no-intervention basis would do, but would not necessarily reflect the stability of the measure with a sub-sample of "abnormal" students. In any event, where standardized or criterion-referenced tests are in use, pre- and post-project measures should be carried out by the same person, to ensure that any bias (particularly to generosity in scoring) or other "tester effects" hopefully will be the same on both occasions.

Instead of a straight attainment measure, some workers choose to evaluate by the deployment of a battery of "diagnostic" tests. Some of these, such as "miscue analysis" in the field of reading, can give useful information with practical implications for teaching and reflect qualitative changes in the learning style of students. However, other diagnostic tests are based on elaborate theoretical frameworks for which there is little sound empirical evidence, and may result in the drawing of no conclusions at all or the drawing of conclusions which have no practical import. Where sub-skills are to be measured as part of an evaluation with "diagnostic" overtones, it is important that the real existence of those sub-skills and their practical relevance to the overall educational process is very clear.

Computer programs have become available to assist the teacher with the management of information about learning in the classroom. Forms of computerized curriculum based measurement and norm-referenced measurement can be both delivered to the student and scored by the computer, which then analyzes the results and advises the teacher of the outcome (and sometimes the diagnostic implications for action). Where such tests have a very large item bank, every test presented to every student on every occasion is different, which not only minimizes student cheating but also enables the tests to be taken very frequently without scores being inflated by practice effects as students get to learn the test content. Norm-referenced tests are of course not as closely tied to the peer assessment curriculum as curriculum-based tests, but can still form a useful measure of student progress in terms of generalization of skills to novel content.

Social and Emotional Gains

If social or emotional gains figure among your objectives for the project, you might wish to attempt some sort of measure of this, although to do so in such an area is fraught with difficulty, and doubts about reliability and validity will be great. Again, consideration is needed of whether these measures are to apply to helper, helped, or both.

A crude naturalistic indicator of improved behavior might be a reduced incidence of disciplinary referrals. There may be evidence of reductions in bullying, fighting and vandalism. Where data on these are not already collected through existing record systems, it may be worthwhile to have adults in regular contact with target children complete some form of rating, or a more specific checklist of problem behaviors, or more generalized observational assessments of problem behavior.

Direct observation with reference to some structured schedule is always valuable, but has the disadvantage of being very time consuming, so it is usually necessary to ask adults to make observations only in times when they would in any event be in contact with the relevant children. Of course, reductions in some of the more dramatic problem behaviors should not be routinely expected. In most cases, it will be interesting merely to see whether peer assessment partners interact with each other more outside of the peer assessment situation for the duration of the project, and at follow-up beyond. Naturalistic indicators such as choice of peers for teams and activity groups can be most revealing.

Beyond direct observation, there are a range of other measures, which may have the virtue of seeming quicker and easier, but which also raise more serious questions about relationship to everyday reality. Some form of sociometry is a particular favorite, on a before and after basis, to discern whether pairs develop any greater preference for each other on paper and pencil completion of peer preference lists. Attempts can be made to tap the more generalized attitudes of pairs to each other, and this could be done verbally on an individual or group basis, or with no fewer threats to reliability via some form of simple questionnaire of controlled readability. Some project coordinators like to use paper and pencil "tests" of self-concept or self-image, but some fairly erratic and implausible results have emerged from such exercises.

With all these measures, the issue of generalization needs to be addressed. Is it enough to have some form of evidence that social and emotional gains have occurred that are specific to the pair or the situation, or is it reasonable to expect these gains to generalize to ordinary classroom sessions, free-play times, or perhaps even to the community and home environments beyond the school boundary?

Behavioral vs. Attitudinal Data

Our discussion of the difficulties of evaluating social and emotional gains highlights a continuing quandary in research of this kind – the inconsistent relationship between what people feel and what they do. In fact, of course, no single kind of data is wholly valid by itself, and it is useful to gather a mixture of kinds of data wherever possible, to obtain a fuller picture of what actually happened in a project from a variety of perspectives. This is known as "triangulation."

Behavioral measures can relate to either the process or outcome aspects of evaluation. They may include observation of required or desired behaviors during the project, in comparison with such behaviors occurring naturally during a baseline period or in comparison with those behaviors occurring spontaneously in a control group. Behavior cannot be observed continuously, and some form of subject-sampling, time-sampling or fixed-interval-sampling might be employed. In these cases, it is important to check on inter-observer reliability. It is, of course, possible to attempt to assess behavioral change in a much looser way by asking observers to complete rating scales, but these are much less reliable and suffer from a "halo" effect.

Methodology for assessing "attitudes" is problematic. The whole notion of "attitudes" is highly nebulous. If you want to analyze people's feelings about the project, ask for them directly, but don't expect them necessarily to bear much relationship to the participants' actual behavior or even the gains shown in attainment. On the other hand, if you want people's observations of what participants actually did, ask for that directly, giving a "no observations made" option. But do avoid confusing the two by asking for woolly generalized "attitudes" or "opinions."

The views of the major participants in the project (helpers, helped, coordinators, and other professionals) should always be elicited. To rely simply on primitive instruments such as tests is to risk missing the texture of the reality of what happened. The participants will probably offer more process insights than summative conclusions, but the former must be actively elicited. Soliciting participant opinions serves not only to gather information, but also to clarify the information giver's mind on the subject, resolve any residual practical problems, and very often to recharge and commit the participants to continued effort.

A group meeting for all participants at the end of the project (or at the end of the initial "push") is often a good idea. This could be audio- or video-recorded for more detailed analysis later (although an analysis of such complex data could prove a massive task). If time is available, individual interviews with at least a sample of the helpers according to some semi-structured format is desirable. Similar interviews with the helped students and professionals are desirable, but should preferably be carried out by an "outsider" to the project if they are to be objective.

Realistically, time constraints and/or the need to have readily analyzable data often drive people into using some form of questionnaire. However, there are very large doubts about the reliability and validity of responses to paper-and-pencil measures. In the construction of questionnaires, the project leaders must decide which questions are important to them, but the device must be structured to eliminate any possibility of leading respondents into giving a particular answer. A multiple-choice format gives easily analyzable data, but is crude and simplistic, while an open-ended format is dependent on the free-writing skills of the respondents and yields data that is often difficult to analyze. A balance between the two is usual. Some overall index of consumer satisfaction is desirable, and a useful acid test is always the question: "Would you recommend the project to a friend?"

Generalization and Maintenance

Are the gains made in peer assessment specific to that situation, or do we expect them to generalize – to other situations, to other (untargeted) skills or problems, to other resource materials, or to other helping or helped students? If we do expect this, how are we to measure it? Most difficult of all, how are we to measure it easily?

The other thorny question is that of long-term duration of gains made. Many teaching programs have shown reasonable results in the short term, but the gains produced have often "washed out" in comparison to control groups at two-year follow-up. So some form of follow-up evaluation is important, preferably together with follow-up of a control or comparison group. Such an exercise is often made difficult by the loss of subjects from one or both groups – "sample attrition."

On the other hand, it is also reasonable to ask how long you can sensibly expect a relatively brief and lightweight intervention to continue to demonstrate an impact on the highly complex and cumulative learning process.

Where Time Series evaluative data on attainment is routinely collected on a yearly basis in school, follow-up evaluation research is greatly facilitated.

Analysis of Data

There is a great difference between statistical and educational significance. Where a very large sample is used, statistical significance is much easier to achieve. Where a very large number of different outcome measures are used, the chances are that one or two will show statistically significant changes irrespective of any real impact of the project. If a project with large samples produces gains which are only just statistically significant, searching questions need to be asked about the educational significance of the results. Was it worth all that time and effort for such a small skill increment?

Particularly if your sample size is small, it may be better to rely on effect sizes as a measure of impact. Take the mean post-test score, subtract the mean pre-test score, and divide by the standard deviation of the pre-test scores. The result will hope-fully be positive! If it is 0.2 or so, there is a small effect. If 0.5 or so, a moderate effect. If 0.8 or above, a large effect.

For those unsure of their competence in statistical analysis, or doubting the validity of the procedures, simple comparison of raw data on scattergrams or graphing of shifts in averages for groups gives a ready visual indication of changes. Certainly, the data is worth summarizing in this sort of way for feedback to the participants, who may be assumed to be statistically unsophisticated.

Evaluation Results Feedback and Dissemination

One of the disadvantages of complex data analysis is that it takes time, and very often early feedback of evaluation results to the project participants is highly desirable, to renew their commitment and recharge their energies. A simple graph and/ or brief table of average scores for the group are probably the best vehicle for this – remember, the results must be understood by the learners as well.

The unreliability of standardized tests makes giving individ-ual test scores to the participants a risky business, and care must be taken throughout not to give undue emphasis to test data as distinct from other types. Any individual scores are probably best given in an individual interview rather than a group meet-ing situation, if at all.

Evaluation results have a number of other uses. Publicity via the local press, professional journals, curriculum bulletins or in-service meetings not only helps to disseminate good practice and help more children, it also serves to boost the morale of the project initiators and participants. The results may be useful to convince skeptics on the school staff, generate a wider interest, and produce a more coherent future policy on peer assessment in the school.

The school governors will be interested, as should be various officers of the State or School District education authority. A demonstration of cost-effectiveness may elicit more tangible support. Associated services such as library services, advisory services, resource materials centers, and so on might be drawn into the network of community support by a convincing evaluation report.

And so to the final word. If you get results you don't like, you'll spend hours puzzling over them trying to explain them away. Make sure that if you get results you do like, you spend as much time and energy searching for other factors outside the project that could have produced them. If you don't spot them, someone else might – and probably will!

The next and concluding chapter of this book assumes you have operated a successful peer assessment project and are thinking about where you go from there – how can peer assessment be developed in your own practice and how can the practice of others take on board what you have learned?

6

Sustaining and Embedding Peer Assessment

Education suffers greatly from short-lived initiatives that enjoy a brief period of being fashionable, then fall out of favor and disappear without trace. It is worrying that some of these initiatives seem to become fashionable even though there is no good evidence for their effectiveness. It is even more worrying that some seem to go out of fashion even when there is good evidence that they are effective.

So, you have successfully completed a first peer assessment project. You have seen worthwhile improvement in a majority of your students, and are feeling pleased with yourself. Great! Now it is time to think about consolidation – embedding peer assessment within the school organization so that it continues to maximize student potential, enduring through whatever political, financial, sociological or other tides that might flow your way – and preferably making it so widespread, durable, and embedded in the system that it will endure long after you have left the school.

Objectives, Applications, and Evaluation

When embedding peer tutoring in the school organization, you need to continue to be clear about the different objectives for different types of peer assessment. Your objectives for a specific project might be in the cognitive, affective or social domain, or some combination. Make sure you agree within the school team on the objectives you want to pursue. Don't let someone else evaluate your project against a different set of objectives! As to the different possible applications, consider using a mixture of cross-age and same-age, cross-ability and same-ability, fixed-role, and reciprocal-role peer tutoring as necessary and optimal to achieve your objectives.

Plan for flexibility. If you work at it you can figure out a peer assessment format or method that will fit into almost any local exigencics: complex organizations, highly structured schedules, lack of physical space, lack of appropriate furniture, poor acoustics, rigid attitudes in adults in positions of power, rigid attitudes in children who have learned to prefer passive inertia, and so on. But don't be too ambitious to start with – many small steps get you there quickest in the end.

Choose your evaluation format and design accordingly to suit your context, objectives and possibilities, or those of others. Consider which formats will suit which subjects, topics, activities, classes, and so on.

You will need to build in some means for continuing review, feedback, and injection of further novelty and enthusiasm. Otherwise, all pairs will not automatically keep going and maintain the use of their skills. And the same goes for the teachers involved in the project. Further, evidence on the generalization of gains to other contexts and other curriculum areas outside the specifically nominated peer tutoring sessions is also important. You are likely to need to consciously foster participants' broadening the use of their new skills to different materials and contexts for new purposes. All of this will consolidate the progress made, build confidence and empower the pairs still further. Publicizing the data might expand subsequent recruitment or attract additional funding.

Rejuvenation and Iteration

Initiating a project (especially in an inert environment) is very demanding in terms of time and energy, although that capital investment is almost always considered worthwhile later. Once things are up and running smoothly, it is tempting to either relax, or rush on and start another project with a different group. The latter is more dangerous than the former – don't spread yourself too thinly. After a few weeks or months most initiatives need some rejuvenation – not necessarily an organizational improvement, just a change to inject some novelty and provide your project with new oxygen.

Fortunately, peer assessment is very flexible and offers many ways for injecting variety and novelty – change of partners, subject topics or activities, format of operation, and so on. However, please do not try to use peer assessment for everything, or you will overdose the learners. It can enhance productivity to give them a rest for a certain period and then return to a modified format not too long afterwards. In any event, close consultation with the students always adds extra momentum to their motivation – even if their suggestions are contradictory and cannot all be implemented, the feeling that their views are valued increases commitment to the onward process.

You might wish to consider to what extent you can give away some of the organization and management to the participants themselves. Obviously, you would need to check on this from time to time, especially with younger children. Of course, you would wish positives to be accentuated and negatives to be eliminated. In this respect, keeping the feel good factor going is important. However, a degree of self-management (which can include self-monitoring) can heighten self-esteem and responsibility and help to make initiatives self-sustaining.

Once peer assessment is accepted and deployed by more staff, some co-ordination will be necessary. Working together, you can build iterative cycles of involvement in different kinds of peer assessment in different formats with all children in role as assessors and as assessees at different times, in a developmental progressive sequence.

A Warning about Customization

Teachers know best about their own schools and teaching conditions. And all peer assessment as explained in this book needs adjustments to the local characteristics. Beyond this, enthusiastic teachers often want to customize or adapt methods, to "suit" their own classroom or children. However, a word of warning is needed. It is only the structured methods described here that have been evaluated. If you customize so enthusiastically that your method no longer bears much relationship to the original, you cannot expect automatic transfer of effectiveness. For all of these reasons, we suggest that – at least for your first venture into this field – you keep to the guidelines outlined in this book (which still needs you to make many professional decisions about what is best for your own class and your own children).

Extending in All Directions

In addition to embedding peer assessment as part of your continuing mainstream practice, you will wish to consider extending it:

- to more assessors and assessees
- to assessors and assessees with greater difficulties
- to other subject areas
- to other classes and colleagues
- to other peer assessment methods
- to involve parents or volunteers
- to collaborate with another school
- . . .

The potential is enormous. But as ever, remember that a modest development done well is better than a large development done badly.

Reaching the Hard-to-reach

In peer assessment programs, the raw material (students) is always to hand (except for children who truant – but even they often turn up for their peer assessment session). You need to find that your own local evaluation gives you positive results. Then the first students to experience the intervention will probably like it – and will be passing the word on to their younger brothers and sisters and other younger students, who will be expecting this to be available to them as they move up the school. Before long, you may find that demand for the intervention is more than you can easily cope with, and that the students are more universally positive than the remaining non-participant teachers.

Many teachers will be worried about the neediest children, whether their neediness arises from a continuing learning disability or from a more transient learning problem. Will such children be able to cope with peer assessment, either as assessees or indeed as assessors? Sometimes, teachers are tempted to exclude such children from a project and have them work with adult helpers instead. However, we do not recommend the latter. All children should have the opportunity to participate in and benefit from peer assessment. Even a pair with a weak assessor working with a weak assessee can learn! The fact that the pair is required to interact will certainly place demands upon them, and these demands will help them to learn.

Developing a Whole-school Approach

There is no better apprenticeship for being an assessor than being an assessee. Many schools with cross-year class-wide peer assessment programs actively promote the equal opportunity and apprenticeship advantages of this model. Every student who is helped in a lower grade fully expects from the outset to become an assessor when in a higher grade. As students are helped in preparation for becoming helpers, any ambivalence about receiving help decreases and motivation to learn often increases. The asymmetry between assessor and assessee is reduced, and the stigma often otherwise associated with receiving help disappears. All the students have the chance to participate and the opportunity to help, which makes them all feel equally valuable and worthwhile.

Sometimes, students who are helped in one subject are simultaneously helpers to students in a lower grade in the same subject. Those who are helped in one subject might be helpers to their own age peers in another subject. Even the most able student in any grade can be presented with problems that require the help of an even more capable student from a higher grade, and thereby learn that no one is as smart as all of us. The symbiosis of the assessor and assessee roles is something upon which to consciously capitalize.

Over time a critical mass of teachers who support peer assessment can develop in the school. Peer assessment builds on students' strengths and mobilizes them as active participants in the learning process. Not only do helpers learn the subject better and deeper, but they also learn transferable skills in helping and cooperation, listening and communication. All of this influences the school ethos, developing a cultural norm of helping and caring. Peer assessment contributes to a sense of cohesive community and encourages personal and social development. Eventually, it can permeate the whole ethos of a school and be deployed spontaneously in many areas of the curriculum – a learning tool as natural as opening a book or turning on a computer. When you see your students explaining to a newcomer from another school or district what peer assessment is all about, and showing amazement on discovering that everybody doesn't do it everywhere, you will know you have got it embedded. Something that begins as an innovation has become a regular methodology!

Share the Project with Other Teachers

Although every working day they are part of a very busy community, teachers all too often feel strangely isolated. Finding time together to have a discussion about anything is difficult enough – and at the end of the school day, energies are at a low ebb for professional discussions. Ideally, time should be scheduled to bring teachers together regularly in mutual support and problem-solving gatherings where they can share their ideas, materials and methods – and build each other's confidence and self-esteem. Peer assessment works very well with teachers, too! Teachers can learn from each other by sharing their experiences in implementing an innovative practice. Maybe, a first step in this direction could be inviting some colleague to your peer assessment session, and then asking their opinion.

Peer assessment allows teachers to put groups together and co-teach with other teachers, as well as to plan, support and evaluate students jointly. If students see their teachers working together – sharing responsibilities in class – they will understand better why they have to collaborate with their peers. If the responsibility of the peer assessment program is shared between several teachers, the program will have more opportunities to become sustainable over the years and become a regular method in the school. And, of course, this is the goal.

Keeping in touch with other schools that use peer assessment could be another good resource. If they are in the same geographical area, maybe teachers can visit each other's school and observe peer assessment sessions, to learn how other colleagues do it. An exchange of experiences between students could be interesting too. If schools are not near, you can use the internet and create a network to share the projects and learn from each other. This is a sort of peer learning, when the peers are whole schools as well as individuals.

Ensuring Sustained Success

How are we to ensure the longer term success of peer assessment strategies? Embedding peer assessment within an organization or larger community requires careful attention to the needs of the learners, the parents, the professional educators, and the wider system. In order for a peer assessment initiative to last and grow, there are some considerations that should be met.

First, the benefits must outweigh the costs for all concerned if the initiative is to endure. For the initiating teacher, costs will be in terms of time devoted, materials and other resources, and the general harassment and stress involved in doing anything new. All of these must be kept as low as possible. On the benefit side, the teacher will need both subjective and objective evidence of impact in relation to the objectives of the peer assessment project. Sometimes we have a lot of *cold* data about project success (test results, questionnaires . . .), but the subjective data is not always easy to gather. Find ways to allow that after being tutors or tutees, enthusiastic children can express their satisfaction. Happiness in learning is one of the teacher's goals, after all. More than that, the whole initiative also has to feel good – have a warm and satisfying social and emotional tone – this will benefit from a little deliberate cultivation.

Parent's involvement in the peer assessment project is highly desirable. This is true not only in order that the parents understand the method, and how their sons or daughters learn playing the role of assessor or assessee. If they are well informed, and have opportunities to visit the sessions to observe or to take part in them, they will value the project and will be another active support for ensuring its sustained success.

No teacher is an island, and the initiative also needs to be compatible with the current local philosophy, political correctness, and mood of the professional peer group and senior policy makers. Fortunately, peer assessment has largely escaped adverse politicization – it is right up there with motherhood and apple pie in terms of acceptability.

A similar analysis can be applied to the other participants – the assessors, the assessees and the head of the institution. They also need minimization of time wastage and harassment, need to feel good about the project, need to be clear what they are getting out of it and what the other participants are getting out of it, and need to be able to confidently assert their support for it in the face of incredulity from their peer group.

Conclusion

Assume you have now read all the book (in whatever order) and can take a moment to reflect on your learning journey. How good did you think you were at peer assessment before you read this book? Have you implemented some of its suggestions? How good do you think you are now? Where will you go next and how good are you going to be in the future? Well, if you are that good, you might want to become an in-service training leader . . .

Peer assessment has been shown to be effective in a variety of contexts and with students of a wide range of ages and abilities, particularly when organized and delivered carefully to meet the objectives specified (although of course this latter is true of other pedagogical techniques). The reliability and validity of peer assessments tends to be at least as high, and often higher, than teacher assessments.

However, any group can suffer from negative social processes, such as social loafing (failing to participate), free rider effects (having the work of others accepted as one's own), diffusion of responsibility, and interaction disabilities – and this applies to other teachers as well as the students. Social processes can influence and contaminate the reliability and validity of peer assessments. Peer assessments can be partly determined by friendship bonds, enmity, or other power processes, the popularity of individuals, perception of criticism as socially uncomfortable or even collusion to submit average scores, leading to lack of differentiation. Both assessors and assessees can experience initial anxiety about the peer assessment process.

Giving positive feedback first will reduce assessee anxiety and improve subsequent acceptance of negative feedback. In addition, students should be told that peer assessment involves students directly in learning, and should promote a sense of ownership, personal responsibility, and motivation. Teachers can also point out that peer assessment can increase variety and interest, activity and interactivity, identification and bonding, self-confidence, and empathy with others. Social factors require consideration by the teacher. When carefully organized, potentially negative social issues can be ameliorated and students can develop social and communication skills, negotiation and diplomacy, and teamwork skills. Learning how to give and accept criticism, justify one's own position, and reject suggestions are all useful, transferable social skills.

Peer assessment is unlikely ever to replace teacher or computer assessment as the main form of assessment. Quite apart from any other consideration, time would not permit the engagement of students in peer assessment for too large a proportion of their working week. However, I hope it has been made clear that peer assessment is about a lot more than assessment – it is also about improving the effectiveness of education generally and developing thinking skills. It is also hoped that peer assessment is capable of engaging students much more effectively in self-regulation and developing other skills relevant to lifelong learning and work. Of course, such long-term developments have yet to be measured, and would be difficult to measure. Nonetheless, the logic of short-term measures and theoretical perspectives indicate that such a hope is not forlorn.

Readers may also be interested in the accompanying volumes: Topping, Duran, and Van Keer (2017) (peer tutoring in reading), Topping, Buchs, Duran, and Van Keer (2017) (peer tutoring and cooperative learning in many subjects), and Duran and Topping (2017) (the principles underlying learning by teaching).

References

Duran, D., & Topping, K. J. (2017). *Learning by teaching: Evidence-based strategies to enhance learning in the classroom.* London & New York: Routledge. ISBN: 978-1-138-12299-4 (pbk). Also in Spanish.

Topping, K., Duran, D., & Van Keer, H. (2017). *Using peer tutoring to improve reading skills: A practical guide for teachers.* London & New York: Routledge. ISBN: 978-1-138-84329-5 (pbk). Resources website: www.routledge.com/9781138843295.

Topping, K., Buchs, C., Duran, D., & Van Keer, H. (2017). *Effective peer learning: From principles to practical implementation.* London & New York: Routledge. ISBN: 978-1-138-90649-5 (pbk).

Index

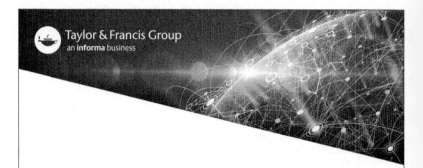

Printed in Great Britain
by Amazon

15712877R00098